Awal  Your Inner Power

How to Discover the Secrets of Health, Happiness and Success

REX JOHNSON AND DAVID SWINDLEY

ELEMENT

Shaftesbury, Dorset ● Rockport, Massachusetts
Brisbane, Queensland

©Rex Johnson and David Swindley 1995

First published in Great Britain in 1995 by
Element Books Limited
Shaftesbury, Dorset SP7 8BP

Published in the USA in 1995 by
Element Books, Inc
PO Box 830, Rockport, MA 01966

Published in Australia in 1995 by
Element Books Limited
for Jacaranda Wiley Limited
33 Park Road, Milton, Brisbane 4064

Cover design by Max Fairbrother
Design by Roger Lightfoot
Typeset by The Light Technology Ltd, Fife, Scotland
Printed and bound in Great Britain by
Biddles Ltd, Guildford & Kings Lynn

British Library Cataloguing in Publication
data available

Library of Congress Cataloging in Publication Data
Johnson, Rex (Rex Ernest)
Awaken your inner power: how to discover the secrets of
health, happiness, and success/Rex Johnson and David Swindley.
p. cm.
Includes bibliographical references and index.
1. Self-actualization (Psychology) 2. Change (Psychology)
3. Mind and Body. 4. Holistic medicine I. Swindley. David.
II. Title BF637.54J64 1995 158'1–dc20 95–12181

ISBN 1–85230–724–2

Contents

Acknowledgements   vi
Preface   vii
What This Book Will Do For You   x
Introduction   xi
The Dynamic Living Principles   xvi

1   What's Life About Anyway?   1
2   You Can Have Whatever You Want   8
3   Why You Are the Way You Are   16
4   The Mechanics of the Mind   23
5   Tuning into Your Inner Wisdom   32
6   Unlocking the Door to Your Inner Self   40
7   Dynamic Mindpower   49
8   The Power of Thought   59
9   Eradicating Negative Thoughts   66
10   Feeding in the Positives   73
11   Affirmations   83
12   Shaping your Future with Creative Imagery   91
13   Getting the Most from Creative Imagery   101
14   The Most Important Judgement You'll Ever Make   112
15   Creating Confidence   123
16   Living Confidently   135
17   The Power Within   145

Appendix: The Dynamic Living Institute   152
Further Reading   154
Index   155

This book is dedicated to all those patients, students, colleagues and friends from whom we have learned so much over the years.

Acknowledgements

We would like to express our gratitude to Colleen Johnson for drafting sections of the text and for her creative contributions and editing; Joanne Figov for her contribution and research; and Pam Hanley and Karen Miller for their wisdom and love.

Preface

What do the wise teachers of the East and great philosophers and religious leaders of the Western tradition all have in common? They all basically teach the same thing – that each of us has a power within, which, if tapped, can help us reach heights previously unimagined. What's more, we all have the ability to tune into this power and remove the blockages that prevent us from achieving our natural state of health, happiness and success.

What are these 'blockages'? They are simply the negative baggage we carry round with us in our minds – the mental conditioning, programming and destructive thinking that cuts us off from our true Source, leaving us with a sense of futility and lack of meaning in our lives.

Our objective is to help you to remove your blockages, reconnect to the Source of Life and become the kind of person you want to be. We offer a step by step approach to removing the harmful conditioning and fulfilling the more than 90 percent of your potential that is probably lying dormant. Once you are able to understand and express the power within you, you will find that you develop a deeper sense of self and that all that is best in life will flow towards you.

Most of us learned many things at school, but never how to live. Basic life skills were ignored, fundamental truths brushed aside. We aim to teach all the things you need to know but were never taught. Our methods are a unique synthesis of Eastern and Western thought based on a total of 45 years of research and experience in education, psychology, health, metaphysics and esoteric philosophy. They incorporate the physical, mental and emotional, combine natural medicine and the latest scientific investigations, and blend the material and the spiritual. *Awaken Your Inner Power* is the first of three books (each of which is self-contained) distilling our work into an easily accessible, written form.

We firmly believe that life is for learning. We've both faced numerous challenges, discovered the potential within ourselves and put it to constructive use. We've already shared the benefit of our experience with thousands of people, including pupils, patients, audiences and workshop participants, both in person and through our books and cassette tapes. We've transformed our own lives, and you can do the same. You, too, can achieve all the health, happiness and success you are looking for.

Note: The English language does not have words that include both 'he and she', 'herself and himself', etc. To get round this, we have chosen to use masculine and feminine pronouns more or less at random. When this occurs, unless the word obviously refers to one or the other, our intention is to include both.

The greatest discovery
of our generation
is that you can
transform your life
by
changing your
mind.

Professor William James

Awaken Your Inner Power is a handbook for transforming your life. To get the most out of it, read it through once, then study each chapter more closely to absorb all the information, ideas and techniques. As they become part of your life, your inner power will blossom and you will find yourself entering a new dimension of health, happiness, success and fulfilment.

What This Book Will Do For You

You will learn practical techniques to:

- Develop your intuition and creative powers
- Discover deep relaxation and inner peace
- Make contact with your Higher Self
- Improve your long-term memory and learning ability
- Find better solutions to your problems
- Take control of your life and find your true direction
- Take charge of your thinking
- Free yourself from the burden of the past
- Improve your health through a positive outlook
- Consciously create the happiness and success you want
- Walk on fire!
- Build a brighter future using creative imagery
- Create unshakeable self-confidence
- Live at one with the Universal Intelligence and express it in your daily life

Introduction

To know how to live is all my calling and all my art.

Molière

The Evolution of a Course in Living

People who consult Rex Johnson about their health problems
are usually in for a pleasant surprise. Not for him the
clinical, standoffish approach of some practitioners, nor the
conveyor-belt style of many modern, 'high-tech' doctors'
surgeries. No, Rex loves to give as much time as he can to
his patients and chat to them while he is working on their
bodies. Ask him about his life, and he's only too happy
to share his experiences with you and relate how they've
shaped his philosophy. Many patients keep returning, long
after they're cured, simply because they enjoy the chat.

When Rex was at school in Cape Town, he was extremely
unhappy and very shy. He was frequently bullied at school
so he left·early and drifted into the printing trade, only to
find that he was bullied just as badly and was still deeply
unhappy.

Then, after being knocked down by a car, his eyesight began
to fade. It became so bad he had to give up his printing job and
take a job as a telephone operator, which he hated. During the
next few months, he often contemplated suicide.

One day, almost on impulse, he went to a talk entitled
'Awakening the Power Within'. As he listened, he suddenly
realized that the ability to overcome all his troubles was right
there inside him and that he didn't have to carry on feeling like
a victim. He resolved that he was going to make the best of

himself and things as they were, so he borrowed some money and bought a disused launderette to build up. It was quite a struggle! Anything that could go wrong did and he worked 14 hours a day, every day, come rain or shine.

A talk on meditation proved to be another turning point in his life. He began practising every day and soon noticed the benefits. Business started to improve, and eventually he was able to open a second launderette, take on an assistant manager and cut his working time down to just half an hour a day.

> *When the student is ready,*
> *the teacher will appear.*
>
> Ancient Hindu proverb

About that time Rex met an elderly lady who introduced him to Eastern philosophy and self-development teaching. She was also responsible for his first contact with the world of complementary medicine, and encouraged him to resume his education.

In spite of his poor eyesight, over the next ten years he qualified in naturopathy, homoeopathy, osteopathy, medical herbalism and nine other healing systems. Meanwhile, he started his first practice. This grew and grew until eventually he bought a large house to run it from and took on an assistant.

Although he was the most highly qualified practitioner in South Africa, Rex carried on studying. He became more and more fascinated by the connection between mind and body. It struck him how often patients would go away cured, then carry on doing the very things that had made them ill in the first place, so that before long they would be back again needing treatment. It was good for business, but not very satisfying. The words of his college tutor kept coming back to him: 'Unless you attend to the consciousness of the patient, you are only removing symptoms on a more subtle level.' He puzzled over the fact that some patients did not respond to treatment no matter what he did, while others recovered almost overnight. He discovered that the word 'doctor' actually means 'teacher'. It seemed to him that it was no use simply working on bodies unless, at the same time, he taught his patients how to live more effectively. It became clear to Rex that:

- **People get sick because their lives aren't working.**

- **Patients often expect a magic formula, but there is no such thing.** They have to have a belief and expectancy that they will get well. If they aren't prepared to do something to help themselves, they won't get better.

- **Health is a by-product of intelligent living.** Only if people's life habits are brought into harmony with their life processes will they recover fully and achieve optimum health.

He was convinced that not only bad diet and lack of exercise could cause illness, but also negative thoughts and emotions. Without taking account of these, doctors were only doing a patch-up job. He'd studied hundreds of books and tapes and attended dozens of seminars, integrating what he'd learned into his holistic health system and passing it on through highly successful workshops and classes in the evenings and over weekends.

After more than 15 years in practice, having seen over 20,000 patients, Rex began to feel that he'd reached his peak in South Africa. He could either remain where he was, enjoying all that his success had brought him (and grow stale) or take a leap into the unknown and expand his horizons. A number of clairvoyants had told him there was work to be done in England, and so he and his family took the plunge and emigrated, settling in Bournemouth on the south coast of England.

Once the new practice was established, he turned his attention to how he could spread his knowledge to help even more people. His thoughts kept coming back to the words of one clairvoyant: 'One day, your writings will have a major influence around the world.' But he was so busy, he couldn't see how he could find time to write anything. The last piece of the jigsaw seemed to be missing.

No army can withstand the strength
of an idea whose time has come.

Victor Hugo

Meanwhile, also in England, Dave was battling with problems of his own. As a teenager he felt inadequate and shy, although he excelled academically and qualified comfortably for university. However, once he had left home, he became increasingly withdrawn and desperately unhappy, and was referred to a succession of counsellors and therapists.

Despite this, he graduated with ease and took a job with a large company where his progress was rapid. But he wasn't finding life the joyous experience he believed it should be. He went through a bitter divorce. Then his personal problems spilt over into his business activities, and he was made redundant. He became ill. No home . . . no job . . . no energy . . . Everything falling apart at the seams. What was he to do?

He began to take more care of his health, became a vegetarian and took up running. He also explored the world of psychology and alternative medicine. He learned self-hypnosis, practised meditation and started to take an interest in his own spiritual development. Driven by the desire to help others, he decided to pursue a career in education and was offered a job teaching business students in a university.

Initially, the world of higher education suited him and he gained a reputation as a caring and popular lecturer, always on hand to help students and other members of staff. Then, one evening he was involved in a car crash and in the following weeks began to suffer pains in his back and neck, and behind his eyes. Still with no solution to these difficulties he accepted a new job in Bournemouth and there consulted Rex about his health problems, Rex having moved to Bournemouth the very same week and started his new practice.

Man's mind stretched to a new idea never
goes back to its original dimensions.

Oliver Wendell Holmes

Dave shared Rex's long-cherished ambition to help people improve the quality of their lives, and they soon built up a rapport. Dave resigned from the university, trained as a hypnotherapist and set up his own practice, and Rex and Dave decided to pool their talents. The Dynamic Living Institute was formed. Through tapes, books, talks and workshops Rex and Dave pass on their Dynamic Living Programme and now aim to help as many people as they can, all over the world. Their dream is that their principles and techniques will one day be taught in schools and treated as an integral part of the curriculum. They want this knowledge to be freely available to everyone.

They hope you will enjoy this book and find what you are looking for. It will give you the confidence and knowhow to tap into the power which is lying dormant within you – and transform your life!

No man can reveal to you aught but
that which already lies half asleep in
the dawning of your knowledge.

The teacher, if he is indeed wise, does
not bid you enter the house of his wisdom,
but rather leads you to the threshold
of your own mind.

Kahlil Gibran

The Dynamic Living Principles

1 You create your own reality with your thoughts, feelings and attitudes.

2 You have the right to a better quality of life: to health, happiness and success.

3 The reason most people get ill is because their lives aren't working.

4 You can transform your life by changing your attitude.

5 Whatever your mind can conceive and believe, you can achieve.

6 Decide to build into yourself the qualities and characteristics you need for success.

7 You can have whatever you want in life, providing you are willing to invest the necessary time, energy and effort.

8 Live in the present moment. Life is a journey to be enjoyed, not a struggle to be endured.

9 Transform your conscious mind with the Dynamic Living Principles and your unconscious with the Dynamic Living Formula (see page 111).

10 Allow yourself to be guided and supported by the Universal Intelligence within and you will always be happy, healthy and successful and have the courage to follow your dreams.

1 What's Life About Anyway?

YOU HAVE THE RIGHT TO A BETTER QUALITY OF LIFE: TO HEALTH, HAPPINESS AND SUCCESS.

Dynamic Living Principle 2

Research carried out a few years ago came to the surprising conclusion that the qualities we need to enjoy a happy, healthy and successful life are the same as those of a five-year-old child.

Do you remember being a five-year-old? Were you carefree? Creative? Bouncing with energy? Fearless? Insatiably curious about everything? Did you have a natural, spontaneous sense of humour? These are all characteristics of most young children before a repressive school system and inept parenting strip them of the imagination, enthusiasm and spontaneity they once had.

At the age of five, you have no self-consciousness or selfdoubt. The world is truly your oyster and you're determined to get whatever you want. Watch any young child demanding sweets from a parent. Are they easily put off? Frightened to ask for what they want? Willing to settle for less? How many young children have to resort to sleeping pills at night because their minds are so stuffed full of worries about the future that they can't let go? How many wake up in the morning still tired because they've tossed and turned all night fretting about some incident in the past? Very few. And yet it's not because a child's mind is less lively than an adult's. On the contrary, a five-year-old's brain is roughly twice as active.

Ask most adults if they value spontaneous childlike qualities and they would say yes, of course they do. Ask if they still have them, and most would have to admit that they haven't. Somewhere in the mists of time they've been left behind. Only occasionally are they able to recapture that happy age of innocence. How? Probably through alcohol. They drink themselves into a stupor and, with their inhibitions dulled, joyful abandonment suddenly seems all right.

Have you ever felt that there must be more to life than you're experiencing? That your talents just aren't being used and your potential as a human being isn't being realized? As you plod along at your job, feeling worn down by the daily grind, have you ever paused and wondered why you're here, and whether life has any purpose? Then carried on with the task at hand, resigned to 'reality', feeling incapable of doing very much about it?

Life is what happens to you while you're busy making other plans.

John Lennon

Next time you're in town, take a look at the expressions on the faces of the people around you. Try leaning on a lamppost for a few moments and watch closely. Are they cheerful, friendly, lit up with enthusiasm? Probably not. Long faces and sullen expressions are everywhere. Observe the way people move. Are they purposeful, energetic, dynamic? Or do they plod along listlessly, seeming to lack motivation and direction? Do you ever wonder how many of your fellow human beings are truly happy and fulfilled? Many seem to muster only just enough energy and enthusiasm to keep themselves going, and reap barely enough rewards to prevent them from giving up altogether. They settle for a barren existence which could not truthfully be described as 'living'.

In an age when we have solved most of the problems that plagued our ancestors, we are surrounded by defeatism and despondency. Depression and alcoholism are on the increase. The hospitals are overstretched, the prison system bulging at the seams, and unemployment has been so high in some areas for so long that some families are into their second or third generation of living on welfare payments. It seems that television soap operas provide the only distraction to an empty existence.

Many people, even those fortunate enough to have well paid jobs, consider their work to be little more than a painful experience to be endured between weekends. They're too busy making a living to design for themselves a fulfilling and satisfying life. Then, after a lifetime of slaving away at a job that offers little interest or excitement, they retire virtually broke, with not much to look forward to but a few desperate years on the breadline.

How about you? Does this picture sound depressingly familiar? Or do you wander along feeling reasonably content? Or possibly you're one of those fortunate people who has managed to find a measure of fulfilment in their life but still feel something intrinsic is missing. If so, you're not unusual. Most of us achieve less than 5 percent of our potential.

Let us endeavour so to live that when we come to die even the undertaker will be sorry.

Mark Twain

Imagine opening your newspaper one day and skimming through the obituaries. You don't normally dwell on this page, of course, but today something draws you to it. It is a description of someone who has recently passed away; not a famous celebrity, but a person who seems much like yourself. The article describes a life dotted with successes and failures, periods of unhappiness and others of joy, things done and left undone, tried and untried. You can empathize with this person – their life was not unlike your own. Then you reach

the last sentence and it hits you like a thunderbolt: it *is* you!
This is your obituary.

Are you happy with what it says? Does it give the
impression that the deceased was a good and loving person?
Was she successful at work? Did others find her company
enjoyable and stimulating? Did she live an interesting and
worthwhile life and leave the world enriched for her having
been here?

Or not?

It might be an illuminating exercise to spend a few moments
reflecting on what you would like to read in your obituary.
And then consider whether what will actually be written is
likely to match your expectations. Then take a minute to
read the Dynamic Living Principle number 2 on page xvi
and ask yourself, 'What would a life richly endowed with
health, happiness and success mean to me? Am I satisfied
with the future I am creating for myself right now, or am I
just going through the motions? What is this potential which
lies within me?'

> *If you deliberately plan to be less than you
> are capable of being, then I warn you that you
> will be unhappy for the rest of your life.
> You'll be evading your own capabilities,
> your own possibilities.*

Abraham Maslow

We've thought long and hard about the recipe for a happy,
fulfilling life, and listened carefully as our patients told us
about their hopes, dreams and fears for the future, and come
to the conclusion that there are seven main ingredients.

- **Good health** – a level of vitality which goes far beyond
  freedom from disease – and has boundless energy and
  enthusiasm for life.
- **Material sufficiency**, which means having more than

enough for your needs and not having to spend time and energy worrying about money.

- **Loving relationships** – most people's number one desire – for which you need the ability to communicate and get along with others, to listen and express yourself well, and to accept people as they are and make them feel special.
- **Being able to live as you wish,** to be in control of the direction of your life, pursuing your interests and talents and making your own choices.
- **A sense of purpose and fulfilment**: a deep inner knowledge that your life has some meaning; a conviction that you know where you are going and how you are going to get there; an appreciation of how you can best contribute to your own personal and spiritual growth.
- **Peace of mind**: the ability to feel good about yourself all the time and to be free from fear and other negative emotions; a genuine liking for yourself; a leaning towards the sunny side of life rather than the shade.
- **The belief that you will leave the world a better place than you found it** and the satisfaction of knowing that you have made a valuable contribution and influenced the personal and spiritual growth of others.

Read through this list again and assess how your own life measures up against it. If you can put your hand on your heart and honestly say you've achieved all seven, your life is certainly in good order. Indeed, perhaps you should be writing your own book – we could definitely learn a thing or two from you! If not, you're selling yourself short. It may sound like a cliché to say that you *can* get what you want out of life, but that is only because it is true. Now what are you going to do about it?

Well, the first thing you've got to realize is that nobody else will do it for you. If you want your life to be transformed, don't kid yourself.

No one else will do it for you ... you have to do it for yourself!

The government won't do it for you.
Doctors don't know how.
The church can't do it.
Other people are too wrapped up in themselves.

But take heart. You are the *best* person for the job and you *do* have the power within you. If you are unhappy with the direction of your life, you can change it. We all live in an ocean of consciousness, surrounded by an infinite intelligence – an energy that created you from two cells, keeps your heart beating, your blood circulating and your food digesting even while you are asleep. Life has a purpose for you. Have you yet to discover what it is? Are you perhaps moving towards it? You might be closer than you think.

This book will help you throw off any limitations and, by tuning into the life force and allowing it to guide you, create a new destiny for yourself. It contains tools, strategies and techniques for taking charge of your thoughts, raising your self-esteem, improving your relationships and realizing your dreams. It will help you to grow mentally, emotionally and spiritually, fulfil your potential and get what *you* want out of life.

We don't claim to have arrived there ourselves yet, but we know that we're on our way. We're fond of quoting an old saying at our workshops: 'It doesn't matter if the signpost is rotten as long as it's pointing in the right direction.' And we're very sure of this particular signpost because we've seen so many of our patients and friends follow it and turn their lives round. You'll meet many of them in the pages that follow, including people like the 74-year-old woman who told Rex, 'I'd been married for 49 years when my husband died. Now I've decided to start living at last. If only I'd known all this 50 years ago, my life could have been so different. Thank you.'

Everybody, yes, everybody, wants health, happiness and success. As you work your way through this book, you'll learn a set of life skills that will allow you, to quote Thoreau, 'to head confidently in the direction of your dreams and meet with success undreamed of in common hours'.

Someone said to me, 'I hope you live to see
all your dreams fulfilled.' I replied, 'I hope not,
because if all my dreams are fulfilled, I'm dead.'
It's unfulfilled dreams that keep you alive.

Robert Schuller

2 You Can Have Whatever You Want

YOU CAN HAVE WHATEVER YOU WANT IN LIFE, PROVIDING
YOU ARE WILLING TO INVEST THE NECESSARY TIME, ENERGY
AND EFFORT.

Dynamic Living Principle 7

How badly do you want to be healthy, happy and successful?
No, this isn't a flippant question; it isn't as silly as it sounds.
Many people would rather make do with what they've got,
because it would be too much trouble to change. About
20 percent are willing to invest the effort to make their
lives work; the other 80 percent live in hope that fate, the
national lottery or the football pools will come up trumps
and offer them a better deal, but they're not prepared to take
the necessary steps to help themselves. We call this the 80:20
rule. It's been researched in many different countries and the
findings are always roughly the same.

The 80:20 rule certainly seems to apply to health. About 20
percent of Rex's patients are willing to do whatever it takes to
get better. These patients are willing to change their lifestyles
to get well and make sure they stay healthy. About 20 percent
of Dave's psychotherapy clients do their 'homework'; 80
percent don't. Guess which group is more likely to complain
that the treatment isn't working?

Within the 80 percent majority are two smaller groups.
About 60 percent would like to be well, but only if the
doctor does all the work and the medicine doesn't taste too
bad. Doctors' waiting rooms all over the world are packed
full of people like this.

Then there are the 20 percent who would actually rather
stay ill or even die. To most people this sounds unbelievable,

but it's true. Life is too much trouble for them and they have a ready-made excuse for every eventuality. Being sick is less demanding, and it has its advantages: they can milk the kindness and sympathy of others (until they get fed up and avoid them). It's the ultimate cop-out.

Sometimes when we make this point, we're accused of being hardhearted, but we're not. We're not judging these people; we're just saying that this is the way they are. But of course nothing is ever written in stone. Sometimes the penny drops and a remarkable transformation takes place. Such a person was a young man named Karl. He was a 15-year-old suffering from depression.

When Karl was six and his sister two, his parents separated after several years of violent confrontation. Two years later, his mother sent him to live with his father (who had remarried) 200 miles away. Although he settled into his new home, he longed for his mother and sister. He saw them every school holiday, but somehow it wasn't enough. Occasionally, he would cry himself to sleep. 'Why can't you and Mum live together like a proper family?' he once asked his Dad in despair. His father was too distraught to reply.

It took three years of patient care to help Karl over the worst of his troubles, and then his young life was disrupted once more. The family moved house and again he went through the pain of leaving people behind.

He took an immediate dislike to his new school. He found the teachers unsympathetic and he was teased mercilessly about his regional accent. To make matters worse, the first boy he tried to make friends with rejected him and joined in the taunting. He felt that everyone was against him, and that life wasn't worth the effort. He started overeating and became seriously overweight. He had few friends, no outside interests and would spend most of his time watching television. On one occasion when his father tried to talk to him, Karl attacked him with an iron bar. This was the last straw. He was referred to Dave.

Initially, Karl was unwilling to do anything to help himself. Everything was someone else's fault; his father, his stepmother, mother, the school, the teachers, his fellow students – seemingly everyone with whom he'd ever come into contact. Those first few sessions were quite a struggle. Then one day, Karl disclosed that he'd once seen a television programme about children whose parents had divorced. It concluded that these children were less well adjusted and were demotivated and far unhappier than the average child. It spelt out the old Freudian hypothesis that the first five years determined a person's pattern for life and that, once set, there was little anyone could do to change it. From that moment on, Karl had come to believe that he could do nothing to help himself, so he had stopped trying.

Over the months, Dave got Karl to see that there was actually plenty he could do. He showed him how his negative thoughts were affecting him and taught him new, positive thinking techniques. He encouraged him to set himself personal goals and work towards them. He persuaded him to change his eating habits and take more exercise. Step by step, Karl began to take more interest in the outside world. He began to believe that he could choose what he wanted to do with his life, instead of having it imposed on him by others. He realized that he could be a master rather than a victim of his circumstances.

Two years later, a slimline Karl had discovered a passion for art and was studying it at college, playing several musical instruments and performing regularly in public. He also had a well-paid Saturday job at a local builders' merchants. He took up sailing, rock climbing and orienteering. He had a wide circle of friends. He was a reformed character – positive, self-assured and optimistic.

DECIDE TO BUILD INTO YOURSELF THE QUALITIES
AND CHARACTERISTICS YOU NEED FOR SUCCESS.

Dynamic Living Principle 6

The point is, this change didn't take place by magic. It took a couple of years of patient and persistent effort by Karl himself. First, he had to make the *decision* to change. Then he had to *build into himself* the qualities and characteristics he knew he would need and, at the same time, *take action*. We're offering you the same opportunity – are you willing to take it? If you want to live an 'average' sort of life, you have that choice. If, on the other hand, you're one of the 20 percent who want to get more out of your life, read on.

> *It's a funny thing about life. If you*
> *refuse to accept anything less than the best*
> *you very often get it.*

> W Somerset Maugham

A Question of Balance: The Five Life Areas

It's obvious, isn't it? A happy and successful life is a balanced life. We've all heard of the workaholic who works so hard he doesn't make time to enjoy the fruits of his labour. As the Bible says, 'What does it profit a man if he gains the whole world but loses his own soul?'

There are, broadly speaking, five areas which, when correctly balanced, cover all the facets of a fulfilling life.

- **The physical and health.** Without health, there is little else. When you are ill, your everyday life comes to a standstill. Serious illness can force you to re-examine your values. Yet most people appreciate their health only when they no longer have it.
- **The financial and career.** Money is a necessity. You need it to pay for everything you want. Without it, you couldn't do much about the other four areas of life. Besides, your career can provide interest and excitement and an opportunity to contribute to the community.
- **Social and relationships.** For most people, the source of

greatest happiness. If your relationships aren't working, very little else will.

- **Leisure and recreation.** It is important to have fun, to relax and to be creative. Too much work and not enough play causes stress. Allow time for hobbies, holidays and enjoyment.
- **The spiritual and self-development.** To live the kind of life you want to lead, you must first become the kind of person you need to be, which means working on yourself and consciously developing the qualities you need.

We examine all five areas closely in this book, but first a few words of warning. If you start off with the wrong attitude, you won't get far, so we'd like to pinpoint some of the most destructive at the outset.

Five Formulas For Failure

We don't claim to cover all the known psychological pitfalls as (unfortunately) they are legion, but any of the following would guarantee failure in any area of life. You can probably add a few extra points of your own, based on your own experience and observations.

1 'I Can't Help the Way I Am.'

Oh yes, you can! From the time you reach adulthood, you are 100 percent in charge of your life. You are the way you are because of decisions *you* have taken in the past. Accept this, as Karl did, and you're on your way.

But if you want to fail, start by affirming to yourself that nothing you ever do will make any difference because 'you're not really responsible for the way you are'. Tell yourself that, in a tragic accident of birth, you inherited a set of insurmountable personality defects from your parents which made it impossible for you to succeed. Of course, you had such a difficult childhood that you never had a chance. No wonder you're like you are. This attitude is a recipe for disaster.

2 'I Can't Change the Past.'

Of course you can't. But you can learn from it and move on. Yes, you probably do have unhappy memories and negative conditioning. We all have, but the question is, what are you going to do about it – keep repeating the same old mistakes, or break free? The ultimate neurosis is doing the same today as you did yesterday and expecting different results. Your negative 'tapes' can be erased and replaced if you're willing to work at it. The past is the past; it remains alive only in your thoughts and will only affect the future if you let it.

> *Experience is not what happens to a man. It is*
> *what a man does with what happens to him.*

> Aldous Huxley

3 'I Know I'm Negative, But I Can't Help It.'

Once again, oh yes, you can! And you must. Negative thinking will kill off any chance of changing your circumstances. It is the cage that imprisons you. Positive thoughts lead to positive action, and negative thoughts lead to negative action or inaction.

Your thoughts are expressed in words and sentences, so it's important to choose them wisely. Avoid words that end in '. . . n't', like 'can't', 'won't', and 'shouldn't'. If you catch yourself thinking, 'Nothing ever works out for me', or, 'It's not my fault, I'm just unlucky', think again. As you'll discover, your thoughts are very powerful and it's very easy to sabotage yourself by dwelling on negatives.

You have it within your power to develop a sense of fun, a positive and optimistic outlook and genuine, infectious enthusiasm for life. What are you waiting for?

4 'Tomorrow Will Do.'

Oh no, it won't. Do you know anyone who follows the golden rule of all procrastinators, 'Never do today what you can put off till tomorrow'? Intimately? You, perhaps? Do you believe that if you ignore your problems for long enough they'll go away? They don't. All they do is accumulate until they seem even more daunting. This can sometimes lead to low self-esteem, anxiety and even depression.

If you just drift through life with the vague idea that one day in the future you'll start developing your potential, you won't make any progress at all. You have to work on yourself systematically and with determination, so set aside some time every day. We recommend an hour a day, not a lot for such a big reward. 'I don't have any time to spare', you might say. 'I already seem to be busy 25 hours a day.' We've heard it all before, but in our experience if you want to badly enough you'll find the time. Time is very democratic: we all have exactly 24 hours a day to do with as we choose.

The first step is always the hardest and the most important, so make a vow to get started and take a step in the right direction. (And if you return this book to the bookshelf without reading it through you've scuppered yourself already.)

The best way to overcome procrastination is to adopt the maxim 'Do it now!' so whenever you feel stuck, say it firmly to yourself and take action immediately.

*The journey of a thousand miles
starts with a single step.*

Ancient Chinese proverb

5 'I Can't Be Bothered.'

Perhaps not. It's up to you. You can choose to let laziness defeat you if you want to, and, make no mistake, we're not offering you an easy ride. You've been the way you are for a few years now, and there are no instant solutions. You'll need self-discipline, persistence and enthusiasm. At times you won't appear to be making very much progress, but you'll find one day that you will look back on where you were, say, a year ago and marvel at the changes that have taken place.

There is a story about Socrates, the Greek philosopher (c470–400BC). One day, a student asked him how he could achieve wisdom. Socrates took him to the riverbank and ducked his head under the water for several minutes. When the student surfaced, Socrates asked him how badly he had wanted air.

'More than anything else in the world,' he replied.

'When you want wisdom as much,' said the philosopher, 'it shall be yours.'

So, desire is the first step. If yours is strong enough, you'll make time to work on yourself every day. Spend two periods of 20 minutes each on the suggested relaxation exercises (see Chapter 6) or, if you prefer, use a specially produced relaxation tape, and 20 minutes exercising or reading inspiring and informative material (see Further Reading) or listening to self-improvement cassettes. (Exercise programmes and relaxation and self-improvement cassettes are available from the Dynamic Living Institute – see Appendix.) It's never too late to make a start.

3 Why You Are the Way You Are

YOU CREATE YOUR OWN REALITY WITH YOUR THOUGHTS, FEELINGS AND ATTITUDES.

Dynamic Living Principle 1

There was once a zoo which kept two adult polar bears in a large cage. Visitors came from far and wide to see them, although, in truth, there wasn't much to see. Hour after hour, the poor bears would pad listlessly up and down the length of their cage, four paces to the left, four paces to the right, four paces to the left ... Sometimes they would rear up on their hind legs, look out at the crowd, then drop back on all fours and resume their pathetic routine. After all, what else could a caged polar bear do to amuse itself?

Then one day, a new keeper with new ideas arrived. He didn't approve of imprisoning such magnificent animals in cages. He thought they should have more space and something interesting to explore. So he built a new pen around the outside of the cage, with trees, rocks, a pond and a waterfall – everything a polar bear could possibly want.

The day arrived when the old cage was due to be lifted by a large crane. As a huge crowd gathered to watch, the offending cage was at last removed. The bears were free to wander around their new home, but what do you think happened? Did the bears take advantage of their new-found freedom? That's right, you've guessed it. To the disappointment of their keeper and the crowd, they carried on exactly as before, pacing from right to left and back again, following the same old routine.

Why didn't the two wild animals relish the opportunity to explore and enjoy themselves? What stopped them? There was nothing physical holding them back. The answer is simple: they had become slaves to their own habits. Would human beings behave the same way? Sadly, yes, many would, and do. You might even know some of them. Although they aren't confined by metal bars, they are imprisoned within a mental cage which is every bit as restrictive. The bars are located in their own imagination, and constructed out of their own negative thinking. To make sense of this, we need to take a closer look at the driving force behind all human experience – the mind.

> *Man is born free, and*
> *everywhere is in chains.*

> Jean-Jacques Rousseau

As recently as a hundred years ago, the mind was still a complete mystery. The study of human behaviour was seen as a branch of philosophy or theology. The great philosophers contemplated the meaning of life from their armchairs without testing their ideas in the real world. They theorized about human beings without necessarily studying individuals directly. Nor were the scientists of the day particularly interested. There were too many things to discover about physics and the natural world. But since the dawn of the 20th century, all that has changed. Freud, Jung, Maslow, Rogers, Watson and the Behaviourists . . . all had explanations of what makes people tick.

Some of their ideas have stood the test of time; others have been discredited by subsequent research and some even sound rather silly today. Psychologists belonging to the various schools still argue bitterly among themselves, but we're going to cut through the confusion and put it in plain language. The truth is really rather simple:

You are the way you are because of your thoughts and your past conditioning.

Although they might have differences of emphasis, no school of psychology would argue with this statement. If you want to transform your life, you must override your conditioning by reprogramming your mind, and you must change the way you think. This, in essence, is what this book is all about. Let's lay to rest one of the great myths about human behaviour: the belief that your personality is in some way passed on from your parents in your genes. Are you a product of your heredity or your environment? This has long been a favourite topic of debate in scientific circles.

A psychologist once said that if you look like your Dad, it's heredity, and if you look like a neighbour, it's environment! The truth? Less than 10 percent of your character is handed down in your genes. Some would say much less than that – perhaps only 2 or 3 percent. So if your life isn't working, you can't blame your genes. Most of your thinking and behaviour patterns are learned, and when we look closely, we find that most of that learning takes place in childhood.

How Childhood Experiences Affect Adult Behaviour

When Alan was in junior school, he was called to the front in morning assembly while the headmaster announced to the entire school that here was an example of a 'stupid, worthless individual who would never make anything of himself'. Thirty years later, in psychotherapy, he realized that the headmaster was right; his life had indeed been a bit of a disaster. But if that's what he was taught to believe about himself as a child, is it really surprising?

*The childhood shows the man
as morning shows the day.*

John Milton

When Rose and her twin sister were little, they were left in no
doubt by their mother that they were unwanted. They were
the unplanned fourth and fifth children in a poor family,
and it was a battle to make ends meet. Much later, as an
attractive and vivacious 40-year-old, she began to understand
why she felt so badly about herself and always seemed to be
under stress.

As a girl, Diane was repeatedly told by her father that food
would always be a problem for her because overeating 'runs
in the family'. By the time she reached 30, she was 3 stone
overweight. It took a prolonged course of hypnotherapy
before Diane was able to change this belief and slim down
to her correct weight.

On a similar theme, John, an obese 52-year-old, had a
compulsion to eat everything put in front of him because,
as a boy, he wasn't allowed to leave the table until he had
cleared his plate.

Childhood thinking patterns become so ingrained that
they're very difficult to shift, and the older you get, the
harder it is. The negative conditioning of Alan, Rose, Diane
and John had left them unhappy, disempowered and unable
to cope. Negative conditioning is like carrying a load of
bricks on your back and dragging a ball and chain round
your ankles – every time you try to swim, you'll sink to
the bottom. Positive conditioning, on the other hand, has
a springboard effect, propelling you forward throughout
your life.

What do we mean by 'conditioning'? It is a term popularized by the Behaviourist school which was founded by J B
Watson in the early years of this century. He believed that
the only suitable subject matter for scientific enquiry was
observable behaviour. To Watson, any talk of 'consciousness'

or 'the mind' was misguided, as neither could be seen or measured, or even proved to exist.

Conditioning is a process of shaping another's behaviour by using reward and punishment. One very famous piece of research that influenced the Behaviourists involved a Russian physiologist, Ivan Pavlov, and his dogs. The animals were conditioned to associate the sound of a ringing bell with food, to the extent that they would eventually salivate on hearing the bell, whether or not food was presented. Pavlov drew the conclusion that human behaviour could also be explained in terms of stimulus and response. In other words, all our actions are a reaction to outside events.

Parents, teachers and other authority figures shape children's behaviour all the time. It is the chief way in which we acquire our attitudes and beliefs about ourselves and the world around us. How do they do it?

When a child pleases his elders, they praise him, even reward him with gifts or special treats so he naturally repeats the behaviour. He learns to link this behaviour with feelings of pleasure. The more often this happens, the more firmly it becomes cemented into his nervous system.

But if he says or does something they do not approve of, he is told off. His parents withdraw privileges or even inflict punishment. This discourages him from repeating the unwanted behaviour, and he soon learns that he has a choice: to conform and feel pleasure or rebel and feel pain.

When we are small, we are very impressionable and our parents and teachers seem like gods towering above us. The brain will believe anything it is told repeatedly, and we take on board every word they say, accepting it as the truth. This is all very well if we are constantly fed encouragement, praise and loving thoughts, but this is rarely so. Research shows that, on average, parents say ten negative things to their children for every positive. The average 12-year-old has already been on the receiving end of more than one hundred thousand negative injunctions (and this is a conservative estimate). That's over 20 rebukes a day. For 12 seemingly endless years.

Perhaps it's almost inevitable. It's not easy to be a parent. Parents have their own problems and preoccupations, and are shackled by *their* conditioning. They are often short of time and most likely to pay attention to their kids when they've done something they don't like. Listen to the way some parents talk to their children. 'No!' 'Get away from that!' 'Stop it!' 'Leave it alone!' 'Do as you're told!' Sometimes, of course, children need to be told 'don't!' in no uncertain terms – after all, young children would soon harm themselves and others if left to their own devices – but more often than not there is no danger. It's for the parents' own convenience, or because they are feeling stressed. We all know how infuriating children can be.

But what effect does this have on the children? By their very nature, children are insatiably curious. They want to touch and explore everything. They don't realize that they are driving Mum or Dad up the wall, perhaps putting themselves at risk or causing unnecessary expense. What goes through their minds? 'Mum and Dad are angry with me. I must be doing something wrong again. They're always getting annoyed with me, whatever I do. It must be because I'm stupid. No wonder they don't love me.' If you're told something often enough, it becomes part of your belief system, even if it's not true. It wears down your resistance. It becomes so deeply programmed into you that you still believe it many years later.

The tragedy is that most parents *do* love their children, but somehow don't know how to express it in ways that leave the child feeling valued, respected and loved. Most parents would be heartbroken if only they knew the effect their well-meaning words and actions have had on their children, but unfortunately it's too late. The past is over, the damage done. Their attitudes and beliefs are so strongly ingrained into their unconscious minds that they continue to think and act negatively for the rest of their lives. They simply can't help themselves and they don't even know why.

The Good News

Yes, there is a good side to this bleak story: every one of your habits, attitudes, beliefs and behaviours has been learned; when you were born, you had none of them. Your conditioning is part of your learning, and anything that is learned can be *un*learned. There are many ways of becoming aware of the effects of your conditioning, challenging the parts you don't like and changing them. And we're going to tell you how. But first, let's take a closer look at the mechanics of the mind.

> *Whatever our upbringing has been, as adults the matter is in our own hands.*
>
> Dr Nathaniel Branden

4   The Mechanics of the Mind

We are what we think, all that we are arises
with our thoughts. With our thoughts,
we make our world.

The Buddha

Is the mind just another computer? Some learned textbooks give the impression that that is all it is, a very clever box of tricks that assesses whatever is going on around it and then reacts. This analogy makes the common mistake of confusing the 'mind' with the 'brain', but they are certainly not the same. Your brain is a small mechanism, weighing about 3 pounds, housed in the space between your ears. Some say its prime function is to keep your ears apart, but it has been known to do rather more than that.

The brain in many ways does resemble a very sophisticated computer, but with one big difference – your brain is far superior to the most advanced computer system in the world. The distinguished author of *Discovering The Brain*, James Watson, calls it 'the most complex thing we have yet discovered in this universe'. A computer that came even close to matching an average human brain, would have to be at least the size of England.

But your mind is much, much more. It is an expression of your divine essence, your spirit, and the Universal Intelligence in human form. You'll never convince a die-hard Behaviourist, of course, because it can't be seen, weighed or measured but, like electricity, we know it's there.

But wait a moment. If we are all carrying that kind of capacity around in our heads, why do so many of us fall short of the abundant health, happiness and success that is available to us? The answer is that we're simply not using our equipment as well as we could. The average person uses less than 5 percent of their brainpower. Imagine what would happen if you used 10 percent. You'd be doubling your capacity.

The brain, then, is the physical vehicle through which the mind operates, but what is the mind all about?

The Conscious and Unconscious Minds

One of the first people to explore the mind was Sigmund Freud, a Viennese neurologist who for a hundred years straddled the science of psychology like a colossus. At the end of the last century, he was one of a number of doctors struggling to understand mental illness. The familiar cartoon depiction of a little bearded man scribbling away in a notebook while a patient lying on a couch tells him his troubles, is largely based on Freud and his psychoanalytical school of psychology.

It was Freud who popularized the idea of the unconscious mind. When he first put forward the revolutionary theory that much of our mental processing takes place below the level of consciousness, his contemporaries reacted with scepticism and outright hostility. How could anyone prove such a thing? But nowadays, it's accepted that the mind can be compared to an iceberg. The part above the surface of the water can be likened to conscious mental activity. The submerged mass, comprising 90 percent, is the unconscious, unseen but powerful. Remember which part of the iceberg sank the *Titanic*?

Freud believed that the unconscious was full of dark, animalistic instincts that wreaked havoc with our psychological wellbeing unless brought into consciousness and firmly dealt with by the rational mind. All our biological drives were housed there: the survival instinct, aggression, sex, selfishness, greed, and so on. Freud was not known for his optimism; he had no time for the spiritual dimension (which Carl Gustav Jung was later to incorporate into the psychoanalytic model) and believed the best that most of us could hope for was to move out of total despair into mild discomfort. Nevertheless, his pioneering work on the existence of the unconscious has provided a solid base for subsequent work. We now have some understanding of what the unconscious is and how it works.

The unconscious houses all your programming and conditioning. It works unceasingly, even when you're asleep. It is the automatic pilot that keeps your motor running, controls your heartbeat, your digestive system and all your vital organs. Can you imagine what life would be like if you had consciously to instruct your heart to beat and your lungs to absorb the oxygen you need to stay alive? The unconscious also contains all your memories, dreams and fantasies and is the part of the mind which generates new, creative ideas, often without involving the conscious mind at all.

Its capacity to store and process information is almost unlimited; all your experiences are filed in its memory banks. It also acts as a safety valve – it's a useful library of detailed information that you don't need from minute to minute – preventing your conscious mind from becoming too cluttered. When you are in your normal, waking state, you are unable to recall very much of it. Sometimes information you need is trapped there, seemingly just below the surface. Have you ever suffered the embarrassing experience of forgetting someone's name, perhaps having it on the 'tip of your tongue', only for it to pop up a few moments later when it is too late?

Some material is so painful, so threatening, that it is deliberately buried in the unconscious – 'repressed'. Repressed memories niggle away and influence your behaviour, playing havoc with your emotional wellbeing. Most of your problems come from material stored in your unconscious but, fortunately, it can be identified and released using hypnosis or, with knowhow and practice, through relaxation and meditation. If this sounds a little daunting, don't worry, it's not that bad. We'll explain everything in the following pages.

What of the conscious mind? It's the part that you're aware of, minute by minute. It perceives your immediate surroundings, chooses what to attend to and reacts. It has thoughts, ideas and images which it attempts to pass through to the unconscious mind. If they are accepted, they will be logged away. Moreover, the unconscious is incapable of making moral judgements; it simply accepts what it is told without question. It cannot criticize or condemn. It just does as it is told.

There is a barrier between the conscious and unconscious (the 'critical censor') which sifts through new material like an attorney and acts as prosecution, judge and jury over the acceptability of new ideas.

Once an idea is accepted by the unconscious, it is extremely difficult to change. In fact, new ideas will not normally be accepted unless they are consistent with previous learning, and this is why conditioning is so powerful. If the two parts of the mind differ, the unconscious will always dominate.

We'll have a lot more to say about the unconscious in later chapters, because it is not your *conscious* attitudes that determine your circumstances, but your *unconscious* ones. *Gaining access to your unconscious and wiping out and replacing your old conditioning is the key to transforming your life*. But, for now, we're going to move on and take a look at motivation.

What Motivates You?

Let's say you've been invited out to dinner and the hostess has prepared a tempting gâteau, soaked in kirsch, loaded with chocolate and rippling with fresh cream. Now, you've put a lot of weight on recently, so you face a dilemma: 'I love the taste of chocolate gâteau, but the pleasure will be short-lived. On the other hand, if I refuse, my hostess might think me rude, and I don't want to upset her. Then again, if I have some, I'll get even fatter, it will clog my digestive system and spoil my complexion. Two minutes on my lips, two months on my hips!'

You weigh it all up and make your choice. Every day, you face hundreds of decisions like this. Why do you bother to get out of bed in the morning? Why be nice to the people around you? Why do you go to work, clean the house, have children or go on holiday? In other words, what motivates you to do anything at all?

A hundred years ago, Freud said we are motivated by only two overriding drives, to procreate and to survive. As we've already said, he was noted for his rather dismal view of humanity and, thankfully, later psychologists took a more optimistic and inspiring view. Jung, for instance, thought that achieving 'wholeness of the personality' was a strong impulse in people, and Abraham Maslow, the founder of the Humanistic school of psychology, considered 'achieving our full potential' a driving force. But more of the Humanists later.

As often happens, the 'experts' have sometimes clouded the issue, because the truth is really very simple. You are motivated quite simply by a 'felt need' and your perception of what brings pleasure or pain. In other words, whenever you have to choose action or inaction, or one action over another, you pick the one that seems to be most likely to make you feel good, to offer the most pleasure or threaten the least pain. If you face two painful choices, you go for the least disagreeable. Most people, it seems, will do more to avoid pain than to gain pleasure.

How do you know which is the most pleasurable and least painful? Usually by referring back to the amount of pleasure and pain you feel you endured in similar situations in the past. Some of this information is available consciously; some of it is locked into your unconscious memory banks where it influences you without your necessarily being aware of it. Once again, your conditioning is at the wheel, controlling you.

But there is another way to make this decision, and that is by deliberately taking charge of your thoughts. It is this ability that makes us truly human. For instance, one of the things which distinguishes us from animals is our facility to choose to do something 'painful' in the short term with an expectation that we shall gain pleasure in the long run. So, for instance, you spend two weeks studying knowing that if you pass your exams, you'll be more qualified and get a better job in the future. Or you save some of your money rather than spend it, knowing that one day you'll be able to afford the things you really want. This is the practice of 'delaying gratification', hoping that future pleasure will more than outweigh the pleasure that you are foregoing now.

The Search for Meaning

To return to Maslow for a moment – the Humanistic school, which he founded after the Second World War, held that there was an even stronger motivating force than juggling the balance of pleasure and pain: a search for meaning and purpose. This school emphasized the importance of spiritual growth, meaningful personal relationships and the ability to exert control over our circumstances.

Maslow himself was very interested in human potential, self-development and understanding. He focused his studies on our enormous capacity for knowledge and creativity. Another member of the Humanistic school was Viktor Frankl. He was interned in a Nazi concentration camp for much of the Second World War where he was subjected to the most horrific brutality. His captors wanted him to perform experiments on the other prisoners, but he refused. They severely tortured him and murdered his close relatives one by one, but still he refused to comply. He later wrote that he realized they could do terrible things to him and his family, but they could never take control of his mind. They could never make him change his attitude or his way of thinking.

He survived the war and moved to the USA, where he became a famous psychiatrist. In his book, *Man's Search for Meaning*, he observes that the people who survived the war were those who felt they had a purpose, a sense of destiny in their lives. This, he argued, is what motivates us at the deepest level; without it, our lives are empty and shallow and we are unlikely to accomplish very much.

Are We Responsible for Ourselves?

If you read Freud, you could be forgiven for wondering whether we have any control over our lives at all. When he made his famous remark that 'We are not the masters in our own house', he meant that we are in the grip of primitive, animal instincts that we can't control. The Behaviourists, on the other hand, thought that we simply respond to our conditioning like robots. Neither took much account of our ability to think and reason for ourselves. Wouldn't it be depressing to believe that we are programmed for life and there's nothing we can do about it?

This, however, is now a rather old-fashioned view which does us a great disservice. Literally millions have overcome childhood disadvantages and great hardship to create satisfying and meaningful lives for themselves. We *do* have the ability, through our thoughts, to mould our circumstances. If this were not the case, there would be little point in striving for anything worthwhile.

> *Individuals create their own unique lifestyle and are therefore responsible for their own personality and behaviour. They are creative actors rather than passive reactors.*
>
> Alfred Adler

The True Nature of the Mind

The mind can't be seen or weighed (although some have tried). You wouldn't be able to find it by dissecting the brain; all you'd find would be a mass of nervous tissue. It would be like trying to find Donald Duck in your television set and discovering nothing more than a few circuit boards and a tangle of wires. And yet we know exactly what it is. It is simply the sum of the thoughts that occupy it. That's all. It's the thoughts you think, consciously or unconsciously.

Now, most so-called thinking is little more than remembering. You're facing a problem, so you search your memory banks for a similar situation from the past. You consult your (perhaps flawed) 'frame of reference' to decide how to deal with your present challenge. But real thinking is different. It is examining the present on its *own* merits, independently of what went before, so you don't get trapped into resorting to solutions which are no longer valid.

What sort of thoughts occupy the mind? Literally dozens. Here are a few examples.

Ideas are mental speculations not yet tested and proven.

Beliefs are thoughts about what is or is not true. To say you believe something is to admit that you don't really know, that you've taken it on trust.

Attitudes are beliefs which are spoken or acted upon.

Emotions are feelings you have when you experience some sort of psychological tension. Positive emotions – such as love, joy, determination and confidence – are those which give pleasure or empower you to take constructive action. Negative emotions – such as hate, anger, guilt and fear – cause you pain and render you incapable of taking effective action.

Habits are conditioned responses that arise from past experience. Each starts with a single thought which is repeated many times until it becomes ingrained into your thinking and behaviour patterns.

Ideals are ideas about highly desirable states; the way you want things to be.

Memories are items of information that have been retained after the original event or thought is no longer present.

Prejudices are beliefs that you hold without having sufficient information; prejudgements made without any regard for the truth.

References are your recollections of things that have happened and your interpretations of them. They mould, alter or reinforce your beliefs.

Rules are the guidelines you use to evaluate your experiences. To discover your rules, simply ask yourself: 'What has to happen for me to feel good (or bad) about this experience?'

You may be wondering why we've gone into so much detail about the mind. After all, you don't need to know what's under the car bonnet to get safely from A to B. As long as you press the right pedals and control the steering wheel you'll arrive safely.

Well, yes . . . but you still need driving lessons to start with and, as any mechanic will tell you, motorists who understand the fundamentals of their car drive with more skill and enable the engine to last longer. That's why racing drivers are well versed about the workings of their vehicles. They know when to pull into the pits for a change of tyres. It's the same with your mind. If you understand how it works, you'll make better use of it, stay on course – and have more fun! We'll be returning to the subject of the mind frequently, because the most fundamental fact about transforming your life is this:

You take control of your life by taking control of your thoughts. Transform your thinking, and you transform your life.

This is the key to escaping from your cage and living a happy, healthy and successful life.

5   Tuning into Your Inner Wisdom

*What lies behind us and what lies before us are
tiny matters compared to what lies within us.*

Ralph Waldo Emerson

One evening during the Second World War, Winston Churchill
was entertaining some government ministers at 10 Downing
Street. Suddenly, without warning, he leapt to his feet and
dashed into the kitchen. 'Quick! Drop everything and run,'
he urged the cook. 'Go to the shelter at once. Hurry!' As
he returned to his guests, a bomb destroyed the kitchen of
Number 10, leaving the diners unharmed.

The artist Salvador Dali had an unusual way of coming up
with ideas for his paintings. He would lie on a sofa holding
a spoon. Just as he drifted off to sleep, the spoon would fall
from his hand on to the floor. The sound would startle him,
and he would wake up and immediately draw whatever images
had come flooding into his mind.

When the physicist Albert Einstein was having difficulty
getting the answer to a problem, he would sit alone and stare
at the clouds for hours. When his mind was completely still
he would ask himself a question. Within a few minutes, the
answer would pop into his head.

What do you have in common with Churchill, Dali and
Einstein? Think for a moment. Have you ever been so
preoccupied with your thoughts when on a long journey
that you suddenly realized you'd travelled miles without
being consciously aware of it? Your body was present, but
your mind was far away. You, like these three great men,
had tapped into your unconscious, inner source of power,
something we all have within us. It's an infallible guide which

has infinite wisdom, greater than you could ever conceive of at a conscious level. Call it what you will – inner consciousness, innate intelligence, superconscious, the Source, your Higher Self – it doesn't really matter. What does matter is knowing how to use it. We call it your 'intuition' or 'inner-tuition'.

Your intuitive Higher Self is constantly sending you messages, 24 hours a day, 7 days a week. If you're not receiving them, it's not because you don't have any intuition or it's not working or ceased to exist, it's because you're not tuned in. It's rather like having a blank television screen. You can't blame the television company, which is transmitting away as usual. It's your set that's at fault. Unless you plug it in, switch it on and tune it in properly you won't get any sound or a clear picture.

In the same way you have to learn to connect with the intuitive powers within you. The question is not whether they are transmitting, but whether you are quiet for long enough to listen and take any notice. Intuition is a small voice fighting for attention amid the hubbub of your daily life. It's like the triangle in an orchestra unable to be heard above the noise of the string and brass instruments.

You've probably already had many intuitive experiences, although you may not always have realized it. Have you ever thought of someone you haven't seen for a long time, only to get a call or letter from them within a few days? This, of course, can also be telepathy, which is tuning into others, whereas intuition is tuning in to yourself. Or have you ever had a gut feeling that something just wasn't (or was) going to work out when logic suggested the exact opposite? If so, that was it – intuition, your Higher Self communicating with you.

I do not compose my music. It comes to me complete.
It is as though my mind is a receptor through which
some unknown power channels glorious music.

Wolfgang Amadeus Mozart

Imagine how exciting and dynamic your life would be if you could learn to understand and tune fully into your intuition. It would take all the dread and uncertainty out of living, wouldn't it? You would be able to forge ahead with your plans, always feeling with certainty that you're on the right path. How marvellous to know that you can rely on it to help you with your decisions and that you will always find the right solutions to your problems.

How reliable is it? The answer is, it will work for you to the exact extent to which you're willing to trust it. If you trust it 20 percent, it will work 20 percent. If you trust it 80 percent, it will work 80 percent. If you trust it 100 percent . . . Have faith and courage in your intuition and it will never let you down. But, on the other hand, ignore it at your peril. If your intuition is quietly trying to guide you in a certain direction, and you choose to disregard it, you could be setting yourself up for a lifetime of disappointment, unhappiness and unnecessary suffering.

Maybe you think that's overstating the case. After all, it takes courage to follow a still, small voice or a subtle feeling somewhere inside you when everything else seems to be screaming at you to do the exact opposite. Sometimes the feeling grows until it becomes overwhelming, almost a compulsion to follow a certain course of action. It can even be the *last* thing you actually want to do. Make no mistake, intuition can create a real battleground in your mind if you are uncertain. You might be perfectly content right where you are, feeling that the last thing you really need is to go haring off discovering pastures new. Only it won't go away.

This happened to our colleague Joanne. She was reasonably happy working as a librarian until it dawned on her one day that she belonged somewhere else, in the very different world of nursing. Before then, Joanne had not been remotely interested in being a nurse, but the feeling persisted. The more she tried to ignore it, the stronger it became, so she put out a few tentative feelers, and several years later found herself working as a ward sister in a large hospital.

But intuition works in mysterious ways, because Joanne's

nursing qualifications proved to be a stepping stone to greater things. They enabled her to switch over to complementary medicine, and when she eventually emigrated to Britain she would not have been able to survive without them before her own healing practice took off.

Successful sports and business people, doctors and healers use their intuitive powers all the time, as do scientists, inventors and millions of people in all walks of life. The most successful people have strong insight; they are sensitive to gut feelings. Whether they realize it or not, they listen to their inner guidance, learn from their 'inner tuition' and apply it in their lives.

For instance, one of Rex's patients, Jack, drives a fire engine. 'Sometimes when we're out on a job and the sirens are blaring and the lights flashing, I'll see a car approaching the Give Way line in a side road and I'll get this very strong feeling. I'll just *know* that it's about to pull out, and that the driver is totally unaware that I'm bearing down on him at about 60 miles per hour. I automatically slow down or give him a wide berth, just as he pulls out into the traffic. I've lost count of the number of times I've narrowly averted an accident.'

How does Jack know when to do this? It's not through conscious, logical thinking; it's his intuition taking over. Can anybody do it? The answer is a definite 'yes', and soon, with practice, you'll be able to tap into your own intuitive powers.

How Intuition Works

You've misplaced your keys. You've scratched your head, searched everywhere (including your memory) long and hard, retraced your steps and you still can't remember where you left them. Then later in the day when you're doing something entirely different, it comes to you in a flash. You left them on the counter in the newsagent's. Where did this inspiration come from?

Scientists now believe that it comes from the right side of the brain using information fed into it by the left. In 1981, Professor Roger Sperry won a Nobel prize for his work. He showed how the brain consists of two 'hemispheres', each with its own specific functions. In the West, this was regarded as an important new discovery, but in the East it had been accepted (and even taken for granted) for well over 5,000 years. How do the left and right brains differ?

In essence (bearing in mind that the terms 'left' and 'right brain' are symbolic rather than strictly scientifically accurate) the left brain is responsible for logical, rational thinking, while the right brain governs the intuitive and creative faculties. The left communicates through the use of numbers and language; the right by means of dreams, symbols and sudden flashes of insight. We all continually use both sides, but most people tend to favour one or the other. At work, mathematicians, computer operators, lawyers and accountants probably use more of the left brain, while artists, musicians and dancers tend to rely more heavily on the right. In some activities, such as creative writing, an interaction of both is necessary and the use of the left and right hemispheres changes so quickly that you cannot tell which is being used in any instance.

Ideally, both sides would work together in harmony, as the spontaneous creation of new ideas is a right brain function, while the left brain evaluates, refines and executes them. But, unfortunately, in Western society, the powerful right brain has become the poor relation of the left. We undervalue and mistrust it, and it's not difficult to see why. You could even say we've been *taught* not to use it. From our earliest days, the school system emphasizes the importance of reading, writing, technology and arithmetic, while art, music and literature are played down. Then when we leave school, our achievements are almost exclusively assessed using written work, which predominantly measures left-brained thinking. Young people who are stronger in right-brained activities are often regarded as less able or slow because their brains simply don't function in the same way.

So if you want the two hemispheres to work in harmony,

you'll probably have to make an extra effort to redress the balance. Sometimes, a moment's insight is worth years of experience or several week's logical, left-brained thinking. But when the flashes of inspiration come, they're likely to be only the germ of an idea, and to require further work to develop. Einstein was an excellent example of someone who could integrate the two sides of his brain and use it to greater capacity than most of us. Perhaps a balanced use of your left and right brain won't turn you into an Einstein, but it will help you to:

- Become more creative
- Learn faster
- Improve your memory
- Solve problems more quickly
- Find the direction you've been looking for
- Contact your Higher Self

How will learning to use more of your right brain give you all these benefits? If you cast your mind back to Chapter 4, you'll recall that 90 percent of your mind works at an unconscious level, and it is here that your intuition is housed. You can access it via your conscious mind, for example by asking a question, and the unconscious will search for an answer. Remember, although we call it the unconscious, the term (favoured by Freud) is not strictly accurate; it's not actually unconscious in the sense that we can't reach it, more that we're not usually aware of it. The point is this: that you *can* gain access to it. You can find out what it contains and feed new information into it. How? By learning to make better use of your right brain. Your right brain is the gateway to your unconscious, your means of tuning into the power within.

The great Swiss psychologist and philosopher Carl Gustav Jung, whose ideas are gaining greater acceptance and respect every year, thought that it went much further than this. He believed that the human psyche could not be explained by the individual's conscious and personal unconscious alone, and that we have access to all the lessons learned by our ancestors down the ages. They are inherited by us, he said, and housed in what he termed the 'collective unconscious'. Whereas the 'personal unconscious' is the storehouse of everything that has happened to one individual in one lifetime, the collective unconscious is shared by all. Moreover, everybody has access to all this material deep within their own minds.

But is that where it ends? Perhaps there are even deeper levels of consciousness waiting to be explored. Experienced meditators sometimes claim to be able to tap into much deeper levels of mind, including the Universal Consciousness or the Intelligence that governs the universe.

A student once asked the teacher, 'How can I find God?' The teacher replied, 'How does a fish find the ocean?'

You are living in an ocean of consciousness of which you are an integral part.

All you have to do to access all the powers of the universe is to quieten your mind and listen.

The spiritual teachers of the East have always known this; indeed, they take it for granted. They have a profound saying: 'A busy mind is a sick mind; a quiet mind is a healthy mind; but a still mind is a divine mind.'

Long, long ago, the four wisest beings in the universe were meeting to decide what to do with the secret of life. They didn't want it to fall into the wrong hands and were particularly concerned that humans shouldn't get hold of it.

'I know,' said the first, 'we'll hide it at the top of the highest mountain.'

'No,' said the second, 'sooner or later they'll reach it and abuse it. Far better to hide it at the bottom of the deepest ocean.'

'No,' said the third, 'one day they'll get to the bottom of the deepest ocean, so let's hide it on the moon. They'll never find it up there.'

'Sooner or later they'll travel to the moon and find it,' said the fourth. 'There's only one place they'll never think of looking for it.'

'Where?' asked the others.

'Deep within their own hearts,' she replied. 'It's the only place they'll never think of looking for it.'

You can learn to access this source of wisdom and knowledge deep within yourself and find the hidden treasures inside. It's really very simple – you just have to relax completely and quieten your left brain. Once you're mentally and physically relaxed, the incessant chatter of your conscious mind slows down. You have a sense of blissful tranquillity and you gradually become aware of the still, small voice within. Anyone can easily learn this technique, and it is the subject of our next chapter.

6 Unlocking the Door to Your Inner Self

*When we are unable to find tranquillity
within ourselves, it is useless
to seek it elsewhere.*

La Rochefoucauld

A patient of Carl Jung once rang for an appointment and was told he was fully booked that day. She was so desperate to see him that she made the trip anyway and found him relaxing by the lake near his home, dangling his toes in the water.

'I thought you said you were booked up all day,' she protested.

'I am,' he replied. 'This is the hour I booked for myself.'

Jung knew the value of setting aside time to listen to his inner voice. From this practice, he wrote, 'You come to realize that the power works through you and then you are on the way to a genuine development of your personality.' He realized that relaxation is the first step to unlocking the door to your inner self. In those days, scientists did not yet understand the reason, but we now know that it works because it quietens the left brain and activates the right. To understand how this works, you need to know a little about the rhythm of your brainwaves and how they vary according to your state of consciousness.

In the normal waking state, the brain vibrates at between 14 and 40 cycles per second. We are fully conscious, wide awake and aware of the external world. This is the 'Beta' state. The more emotionally aroused a person is, the faster the vibration. Excitement, anger, fear, nervousness, poor concentration and so on are all signs of an overactive brain.

Between 8 and 14 cycles per second is a zone of relaxation, a serene, sleep-like, dreamy state. These are 'Alpha' waves. You become less aware of your body. You lose track of time. Your thoughts slow down. At this level, the two halves of the brain are in balance and you are in touch with the deeper levels of your mind.

When we enjoy a deep, comfortable sleep, the brain's rhythm slows to 5–8 cycles per second. This is the 'Theta' state, also associated with very deep relaxation and meditation. In the 'Delta' state of deepest sleep and total unconsciousness, the brain operates at below 5 cycles per second.

The Alpha level is the most important for our purposes. 'Going into Alpha' is the mental equivalent of changing down a gear when you want extra power to get up a steep hill. Here lies the rhythm of good health and emotional and mental calm. You also become more focused, and your immune system is strengthened, so your body is better able to heal and revitalize itself. Learning to slip into this wonderful, restful state is essential to your wellbeing, which is why we are devoting a whole chapter to it. Of course, we're talking about something a little beyond settling down with a drink or watching the television. Deep relaxation, the kind which allows your mind to drift into Alpha level and gets rid of all the negative baggage you are carrying, is the key to creative and intuitive living.

The Alpha state of consciousness is so pleasurable that many people have spent huge sums of money on expensive gadgetry which promises to make it a quick and easy ride, but this is quite unnecessary, as are some of the ceremonies and rituals practised by certain 'new age' cults. All it takes is a little knowhow and lots of practice. Then you can take advantage of the benefits of deep relaxation which have been identified since the early 1900s by doctors and psychologists. These include:

- Greater tranquillity and peace of mind
- Enhanced energy and vitality
- Improved digestion
- Lower blood pressure and slower heart rate

- More relaxed muscles, better posture, freedom from aches and pains, including headaches
- Greater clarity of thought and ability to concentrate
- Improved immune function and freedom from disease
- Deeper, more satisfying sleep
- Improved capacity to handle stress and problems
- Improved ability to handle relationships
- More highly developed intuition and creativity.

Learning to Relax

There are many types of relaxation, but we shall outline the three main ones. It's best to try them all and decide for yourself which suits you. A selection of relaxation tapes which can help is available from the Dynamic Living Institute (see Appendix).

Before you try any of these methods, prepare yourself as follows:

- Either lie down or sit in a comfortable chair
- Make sure your head, neck and shoulders are supported
- Dim the lights
- Unplug the phone and ask others to leave you in peace.

Don't try too hard – relaxation is a passive, not an active, process.

Differential Relaxation

This involves tensing specific groups of muscles and then relaxing them, to the rhythm of your breathing.

Breathe in, tense your feet for five seconds. Breathe out and relax. Breathe in, tense your lower legs for five seconds. Breathe out and relax. Do the same with your thighs, and work your way through the muscle groups – buttocks, stomach, back, chest, upper and lower arms, hands, shoulders and neck, until your whole body has been systematically tensed and relaxed.

When you are completely relaxed, count yourself down from ten to one, allowing yourself to let go a little more with each number, so as to deepen the relaxation. One way is to imagine yourself floating down ten steps into a beautiful garden and settling into a comfortable reclining chair, basking in the warm sunlight and listening to the gentle sound of running water or a slight breeze rustling the leaves of the trees. Or you might prefer to picture yourself lying on a beach, or in the country, or on a hillside. Some people like to create a sanctuary in their minds complete with the colour scheme and furniture of their choice. The options are almost endless, but as long as you choose somewhere that you associate with peace and tranquillity, it doesn't really matter.

Progressive Relaxation

Make sure you are comfortable, close your eyes and begin to focus on your breathing. Inhale and exhale through your nose, breathing easily and naturally, and each time you breathe out allow more of the tension to leave your body.

As you begin to feel yourself unwind, focus your mind on various parts – lower legs, thighs, buttocks, back, chest and so on – until your whole body is fully relaxed. As you inhale, say the word 'in' to yourself quietly, and as you exhale, say 'out'. Focus on a specific area as you do this. Tell yourself to relax more and more with each breath. Then, to deepen the relaxation, you can try one of the following:

- Slowly count backwards from ten to one. With each count, allow yourself to feel heavier and more relaxed.
- Imagine descending a winding staircase. Feel more relaxed with each step you take and then enter a beautiful garden, or settle down on a sofa in the cosy front room of a country cottage with a warm fire, and heavy curtains shutting out

the cold. Listen to the rain beating on the windowpanes. Feel safe, secure and very, very relaxed.
• Count yourself down ten steps on to your imaginary beach, garden or favourite patch of countryside.

To return to normal waking consciousness, simply count slowly from one to five, gradually becoming more alert. At the count of five, open your eyes, gently move your arms and legs, get up slowly and breathe normally.

Autogenics

In Germany in the early 1900s, Dr Johannes Schultz developed a system of relaxation known as Autogenic Training, which involved using self-suggestion to induce a feeling of warmth and heaviness in various parts of the body. Physiological changes were dramatic. Schultz used this method to help patients heal themselves, and it has been used in certain hospitals in the treatment of cancer and other serious illnesses. Patients go into Alpha level and learn to use creative imagery. (You'll learn how to do this in Chapter 13.)

For the moment, we shall confine ourselves to outlining the technique. Get comfortable and close your eyes. Allow each part of your body to feel heavy, warm and relaxed. Be aware of the pleasant feeling this gives you. Then silently and slowly say the following phrases to yourself, three times, in sequence. It's a good idea to read the entire procedure on to tape so that you can use it any time you wish.

> *My right arm is heavy and relaxed (x3)*
> *My left arm is heavy and relaxed (x3)*
> *My arms are heavy and warm (x3)*
> *Warmth is flowing into my hands (x3)*
>
> *My right leg is heavy and relaxed (x3)*
> *My left leg is heavy and relaxed (x3)*
> *My legs are heavy and relaxed (x3)*
> *My feet are warm and relaxed (x3)*

My right arm is heavy, warm and relaxed (x3)
My left arm is heavy, warm and relaxed (x3)
My right leg is heavy, warm and relaxed (x3)
My left leg is heavy, warm and relaxed (x3)
My whole body is heavy and relaxed (x3)

My body is heavy, warm and relaxed (x3)
My heartbeat is strong, calm and regular (x3)
My breathing is calm and regular (x3)
My breathing is even and rhythmic (x3)
It breathes me (x3)

My solar plexus is warm and relaxed (x3)
My forehead is cool and calm (x3)
I am at peace (x3).

Now slowly count back from fifty to one, going deeper and deeper into relaxation each time you exhale.

It is a good idea, when you are in Alpha, to 'programme' your mind to allow you to enter the same state quickly and easily at will. This can be done by putting the tips of your thumb and forefinger together and reciting: 'When I put my thumb and forefinger together, and repeat the word "Alpha" I shall easily and instantly go into Alpha.' This is called a trigger, and you can activate it by making yourself comfortable, repeating the word 'Alpha' and putting your fingers together as described, whenever you wish. Once you've mastered these techniques (or at least the one that appeals the most to you), and are able to know instinctively when you've achieved a deep level of relaxation, you can use one of the following quick methods as a shortcut.

Quick Relaxants

Breathing and relaxation go hand in hand. When you are anxious, your breathing is shallow and quick. When relaxed, it is slow and deep. Try this: walk for four steps and breathe in as you do so; hold your breath for four steps and then breathe out for four steps. In time, increase to five steps, then six, seven, eight . . . as many as you can manage. Do this regularly; it has a calming effect and helps focus you in the present. Four more ways of relaxing quickly which involve breathing are as follows.

1 Quick Release of Tension

Take three very slow, deep breaths. Breathe out slowly, saying the word 'relax' or 'calm' softly, until your lungs are empty. Breathe normally for a few breaths. Then repeat the three slow, deep breaths. When you return to your other activities, you will feel calmer and more relaxed.

2 Breathing in a Cloud

Focus on your breathing, making sure it is calm and regular. Imagine that as you breathe in, a cloud of peace and tranquillity fills your body and is expelled when you breathe out. Imagine the cloud having a beautiful colour of your choice.

3 The Sigh Breath

Breathe in deeply, filling your entire lungs. Pause for a few seconds. Then exhale in the form of a long, slow, audible sigh, making an extended 'aaaaaah' sound as you do so. Feel the tension leaving your body, and notice especially the calming effect of the sigh breath on your emotions.

4 The Countdown into Relaxation

Be passively aware of your breathing. With each out-breath, count down from ten to one, allowing yourself to feel heavier and more relaxed. Notice the tension melting away with each count.

You can also drift down into a slightly deeper level of consciousness without necessarily putting 20 minutes aside for planned relaxation sessions, and these are often the most rewarding of all. Spending time in nature is one way. Have you ever been on a long walk in the country and suddenly realized you've walked for over an hour and not really noticed your surroundings because your mind was far away? Trees and rivers are very relaxing. The stillness and the gentle sounds of nature quieten the mind and make it more receptive to intuitive guidance and information. Listening to relaxing music is another. We recommend the slower music from the Baroque classics (such as Vivaldi, J S Bach, Corelli), but choose any that has the desired effect for you.

Another way is to watch your posture. Make it a habit to extend your head upwards, drop your shoulders and relax your body. Try to get your ears, shoulders and hips in a line. Your body will then be balanced, and you will be more able to focus your attention on the present.

Of course, all these methods take practice, and it's a good idea to fill in the odd spare moment with mini-relaxation and awareness exercises whenever you can. This will help to reinforce your relaxation habits and make the exercises a natural part of your routine. It will also do a lot to improve your intuitive and memory skills. So, for instance, if you're waiting in a queue or a traffic jam, instead of getting yourself into an impatient knot, systematically relax various parts of your body until your mind is quiet and receptive. Be aware of what's happening around you and within you. And when you're out walking, practise your rhythmic breathing exercises.

Over the years, we've taught relaxation techniques to thousands of people at workshops and in our practices, and used them ourselves. More and more doctors are also beginning to recognize the benefits of deep relaxation; at a recent seminar, one doctor stated that it could relieve 80 percent of the causes of stress-related illnesses. The benefits can be literally life changing. For instance, Kate, who attended one of our seminars, told us that she had gained such an insight by using these principles that her whole life had turned around. She was feeling healthier, less stressed and more positive, and had recently started a new job which she was enjoying enormously.

One word of warning, though. Simply reading and absorbing this material will not get you the results you want, because the key to any kind of personal growth, spiritual or otherwise, is to take consistent *action*. It takes 28 days to change a habit for good, and getting to Alpha quickly and easily is absolutely fundamental to your progress. So, decide now to get into the habit of deeply relaxing your body and mind twice a day, using whichever method works best for you. Practise the quick relaxation techniques until you've mastered them. In the next chapter, you're going to learn how to make further use of your new skills.

7 Dynamic Mindpower

To do great work a man must be very
idle as well as very industrious.

Samuel Butler

When Thomas Edison, the greatest inventor of them all, was asked where he got his ideas from, he replied, 'I simply pluck them out of the air.' What he actually meant was that he had a novel way of finding answers to seemingly insoluble problems. He would sit quietly for a while, usually when he was tired, holding something small in his hands, such as a few nuts. When he was totally relaxed, his hands would automatically open and the objects would fall to the ground. Edison found that ideas would then come flooding to the surface of his mind.

Another inventor, Elmer Gates, became a millionaire by taking designs that others had abandoned and making them work. He would examine them closely and formulate some questions about them in his mind. He then instructed his staff that he was not to be disturbed and sit in a darkened room for up to three hours, patiently waiting for answers to pop into his head. (He was always careful to have pen and paper to hand so he could jot down the answers before he returned to normal waking consciousness.) The technique seldom failed. When asked where he got his ideas from he said, 'I tune into my own unconscious, the collective unconscious and the Universal Consciousness.'

Although unusual, Gates' method was not new. Oriental sages have used it for millennia, and Christians down the ages have testified to the power of prayer and meditation. The reason why it is seldom practised in the West is that silent reflection has been out of fashion for a few hundred years, although is now making a comeback. For instance, Napolean Hill stresses it in his masterpiece, *Think and Grow Rich*, and Ron Holland, author of *Talk and Grow Rich*, recommends making a habit of sitting down and doing nothing when you are facing an apparently impossible situation in order to allow your unconscious (or your Higher Self) to come up with some solutions. Holland makes the startling claim that:

> *The formula you need for all the wealth, success and achievement, and peace of mind, indeed for all the answers to your problems, and I mean* all, *is* sss
> – Silence, Stillness, and Solitude.

Thomas Edison once remarked to a friend, 'When you become quiet, it just dawns on you'. Why? Because when you are in a state of deep relaxation and mental calmness (that is, in Alpha level) you have direct access, via the right brain, to your unconscious (intuitive) mind. Through your unconscious mind you have a link to the collective unconscious and the Universal Intelligence which have all the answers to any question you could ever ask. So how are you going to make use of this dynamic mindpower? Naturally, we've a few suggestions.

Sitting for Ideas

If you're facing a difficult dilemma, you don't necessarily have to resort to confining yourself to a darkened room for three hours. Rather than continuing to wrestle with it, formulate some key questions, relax into Alpha, ask a question of your intuitive right brain and wait. You will often receive your answer while you are still in Alpha, but if this doesn't happen, don't think it hasn't worked for you. Your inner self will continue to grapple with the problem long after you've turned your attention to something else, so give it time. You might have a flash of inspiration much later when you are doing the washing up, lounging in the bath, ironing or driving your car. You might even come across something in a book or magazine which rings a bell – could this be your Higher Self directing you? Once you've tuned in, you will be guided to the right information, no matter how accidental it may seem. The force works in mysterious ways its wonders to perform!

*A hunch is creativity trying
to tell you something.*

Frank Capra

When you've received an answer that feels right to you, be sure to *write it down*. You may be convinced you'll remember, but don't take the chance. Also, be open to the possibility that more may come your way. There is rarely only one right answer: you may have a choice. If you can't decide, go back into Alpha for more guidance.

In the modern world, there is a great demand for the instant everything, including the instant answer. We are appraised according to our ability to 'think on our feet'. If, for instance, a politician says she can't answer a question and would prefer to go away and think about it for a few days, the chances are the electorate would regard this as an example of dithering or even deviousness. Yet this is usually the best way to handle a difficult situation. Instant answers often come from the left brain, whereas, given time, better solutions would be forthcoming from the right.

Many people, such as the philosopher Bertrand Russell, know this instinctively. When he was planning to write a book, he would collect as much material as possible, mull it over for a while, then put it aside for a few weeks. He always set himself a deadline, and on the appointed day, he would take out the file, sift through the ideas and begin writing. Words and sentences would flow into his head as if by magic, but in reality, of course, it was the result of a lot of hard work. Although his attention had turned to other things, his unconscious had carried on working on the book.

> *The thoughts that come often unsought, and,*
> *as it were, drop into the mind, are commonly*
> *the most valuable of any we have.*
>
> John Locke

If you want to use this approach, remember three things.

- Think about the problem and write down all the solutions that come into your head.
- Decide there and then which day you will pick up the problem again. Then set it aside. (You can always add to your notes if a good idea comes to you in the meantime.) Your unconscious will be aware of the deadline, so trust it. It will continue to work on the problem for you.
- On the given day, go back to it and, if possible, keep going until you have finished the task.

Sleeping On It

This uses the same principle. When you go to bed at night (preferably just as you're dropping off to sleep), ask your inner self for the answer to a question. You might find that you wake up knowing exactly what to do.

This method was used by Elias Howe, the inventor of the sewing machine. He couldn't quite figure out how to get his idea to work, and he spent a long time chewing over this problem, especially late at night. Then he realized he was having the same dream every night. He was being chased by tribesmen on an island and they were throwing spears, which never quite reached him. This was because ropes were tied through the front of the spears, which pulled them back just before they got to him. Of course! He had to put the eye of the needle at the *front*. He tried it, and the rest is history.

Dispensing with your Alarm Clock

Are you one of those people who hates that dreaded moment when the alarm clock bursts into life each morning? Well, you can dispense with your clock by setting your mental alarm. Before you go to sleep, tell yourself that you will awake at the right time feeling rested and full of energy. After a few days, you will find yourself waking up each day at precisely the right moment.

Dave has used this method for years. He wakes up each morning just in time for the sports news on the radio!

How to Recognize your Intuition

At our workshops, we're frequently asked how you can recognize your intuition. How do you know whether the small voice in your head comes from your left brain or your right? Is it your conditioning or a flash of insight? Quite frankly, it's not always that easy, since intuition works in mysterious and subtle ways. You have so many voices in your head chattering away simultaneously – which one should you listen to?

The best way is to ask yourself which one *feels* right. Which, if followed, would provide you with the greatest sense of wellbeing, of satisfaction and peace of mind? Which would give you most self-respect? The stronger the feeling of contentment and fulfilment, the more likely it is to be your intuition.

Very rarely do we experience what happened to Archimedes nearly three thousand years ago. He had, you will remember, been working on a difficult problem for some time, with little success. One day, according to the legend, he was lounging in his bath and the solution suddenly came to him. 'Eureka!' he cried, leaping out of the water. 'I've got it!'

Often, intuition reveals itself little by little in seemingly random incidents. One day, you look back and realize 'that was my intuition at work'. Situations, events and opportunities somehow conspire to shunt you in the right direction. When Rex damaged his eyes, at first he felt desperate. 'Looking back,' he says, 'I now realize that even in my darkest moments I was being guided, and that through all the adversity I was brought to where I needed to be and shown exactly what I needed to do. No sudden flashes of insight lit up the sky, but then it dawned on me that I was slowly being drawn into a new world. I was meeting a completely different set of people, and each one took me a little further along a brand new path.'

If there are lessons you need to learn, your intuitive Higher Self will make sure you learn them. It will place you in appropriate situations and, if the lesson doesn't hit home first time, keep repeating them until you get the point. They say that opportunity often comes disguised as problems, but the trick is to see problems for what they really are, and make them work *for* you rather than against you.

Rex realizes that those difficult times enabled him to discover his innate power. You, too, have the power within you – just learn how to use it.

Memory

You already have a perfect memory. It is a thousand times more powerful than you imagine, but most of it is lying buried deep within your unconscious mind. It is simply a matter of knowing how to dip in and bring the material back into consciousness when you need it. No, this isn't an exaggeration; it's been proven and accepted by leading scientists and psychologists for nearly half a century and Eastern mystics for thousands of years.

For instance, in the early 1950s, Dr Wilder Penfield conducted a series of experiments which involved touching the temporal cortex of the brain with a probe carrying a weak electric current. He used the probe on patients who were fully conscious under local anaesthetic, and they were suddenly able to recall incidents from childhood in great detail. One middle-aged woman relived her fifth birthday party. She was opening her presents and making a wish as she blew out the candles on her cake. She could even name all the guests even though she 'saw' them as little girls whom she hadn't seen for many years. The other patients also relived their memories, experiencing the sights, sounds and emotions they had first felt all those years ago. Dr Penfield had stumbled on to a real hot potato; for the first time, he had demonstrated scientifically that no memory is ever lost.

The brain has an infinite capacity to store information and it retains everything that you have ever seen, heard, felt, tasted, touched or imagined. It's all there, and to access it you don't need an electric probe, just a little determination and the ability to relax into Alpha level.

I feel assured there is no such thing as ultimate forgetting; traces once impressed upon the memory are indestructible.

Thomas De Quincey

Improving your memory is not as difficult as you might at first think. There was a report on the television recently of a woman who had 'permanent' memory problems after falling off a horse and landing on her head. She couldn't remember her past and quickly forgot any newly acquired information. Until, that is, she met a man who specialized in memory training. He taught her the 'weaving a story' technique.

Let's suppose you want to remember a shopping list. The technique involves picturing the items in a funny situation, the more ludicrous the better, and building a story around it. The idea is that a funny story will be easy to remember and the shopping items will automatically spring to mind.

This technique certainly helped the woman concerned, but

we can also highly recommend some others which are based
on deep relaxation.

- Relax completely until your mind is still and you're in
Alpha level, and repeat the following affirmation:

'I have perfect memory and concentration. Therefore I can
recall instantly and easily whatever I hear, read or study. I
remember at will whatever I require. I am at one with, and
have access to, the source of all knowledge.'

Repeat this whenever you're in Alpha level and your
memory will soon start responding to this reconditioning.

- You can easily absorb a lecture or the contents of a book
when in Alpha. Simply relax (using any of the quick
methods we've described) then use the thumb and finger
technique as a trigger, and listen to the lecture or read the
book. Later, when you want to recall any part of it, repeat
the trigger, saying the word 'Alpha', and you'll find that all
the information comes flooding back to the surface.
   This might all sound a bit like waving a magic wand and
saying 'abracadabra', but it really does work. For instance,
a resourceful young student used this technique and got
91 percent in his science examination. The examiners
thought he must have been cheating, and failed him.
'This is impossible!' they proclaimed at the subsequent
appeal, but the student offered to retake the exam in their
presence. This time, he did even better and several red-faced
examiners were left eating humble pie.
- If you are ever put on the spot, for instance to remember
a name or telephone number in a hurry, it is worth trying
the thumb-and-finger technique, quietening your mind and
then asking the question. The answer will often pop into
your head.
- Whenever you are trying to find something you've misplaced, use the same technique to take your mind back to
when you can last remember seeing it. Eventually you will
be 'led' to where you actually left it.

Accelerated Learning

Dave was recently contacted by an 18-year-old student, Steve, who was worried about his forthcoming examinations. He admitted that he'd done very little work but, with less than a month to go and a university place at stake, he was willing to do whatever was necessary to get good grades.

Dave taught him some advanced memory techniques and coached him in accelerated learning methods first developed behind the Iron Curtain in the 1960s and 1970s. Dr Georgi Lozanov, a Bulgarian psychiatrist, used autogenic conditioning and soothing Baroque music to speed up the learning process with students. Once deeply relaxed, he would recite the information they needed at a slow, rhythmic pace. This very neatly cut out all the stress and tension which creates learning blockages and doubled the capacity of the brain to learn because it allows the right brain to play its part.

Schoolchildren in Eastern Europe and the USA have been using these methods to learn foreign languages for years, sometimes to fluency in just a few months. They put their heads on their desks, close their eyes and drift off while a teacher recites the information at the prescribed speed and rhythm. In some cases, they learned more than a hundred times faster than before!

Steve was told to prepare a précis of the information he thought he would need in the exam, record it on to cassette tape and listen to it frequently while in Alpha, especially last thing at night. He recited the memory affirmation and learned the thumb-and-finger technique. On the day of his exam, he used quick relaxation methods to relieve tension.

A few weeks later Steve called to say thank you. He'd achieved the grades he needed to get into university. He felt he'd cheated the system, but he hadn't really. He'd just found a way to make his mind work better, and surely that's what it's all about.

Now that you know you can tap into your intuitive and creative powers and even contact the Universal Intelligence by relaxing your body and mind, you're at the dawn of a new era of self-discovery. Life will become more exciting, rewarding and enjoyable. The techniques you've learned in the last three chapters are well worth practising and perfecting, because once you have done so, you'll be well on the way to transforming your life.

8   The Power of Thought

YOU CAN TRANSFORM YOUR LIFE BY CHANGING YOUR ATTITUDE.

Dynamic Living Principle 4

Science fiction fans are no strangers to alien life forms who can move objects around, transform themselves and imprison their enemies in invisible jails consisting of nothing more than thought energy. Sounds fantastic, doesn't it, yet amazing things do happen: spoon bending, spiritual healing, water divining . . . conventional science grudgingly accepts their existence but can't explain any of them. Yet these are trivial compared to some of the feats achieved by masters of the Orient. What is this power they're tapping into? More importantly, is it available to all of us?

Of course it is, and most of us are using it constantly without ever realizing it. The only difference is it's not so obvious and it takes a little longer. Even as you read this, your thoughts are directing your actions and are determining what will happen to you in the future. Just consider for a moment.

- Experiments using biofeedback equipment have demonstrated that your every thought affects every cell in your body.
- Other people can 'sense' your thoughts and feelings through your aura, which is the field of electromagnetic energy that surrounds you.
- This means that your unspoken thoughts can attract or repel other people.
- Every emotion that you have ever experienced began as thoughts, which, if repeated often, become locked into your nervous system.

Two hundred years ago, Thomas Carlyle observed that: 'It is a mathematical fact that the casting of this pebble from my hand alters the centre of gravity of the universe.' It's sobering to reflect that he could also have written, with equal validity, that 'the casting of a single thought from my consciousness alters the destiny of the universe'.

There's no getting away from it, thoughts have energy. This was spelt out a few years ago by Earl Nightingale. He reminded the Western world of the secret of life with just six words. This line has enabled millions to transform their lives for the better:

You become what you think about.

It wasn't an original idea: philosophers down the ages have disagreed about many things, but never this. For example, the Roman philosopher Marcus Aurelius said, 'A man's life is what his thoughts make of it.' The Bible says, 'As a man thinketh in his heart, so is he.' And, many centuries later, William Shakespeare wrote, 'Nothing is either good or bad, but thinking makes it so.'

What were these great writers and teachers telling us? Clearly they were saying that *you are constantly creating your own circumstances by the way you think*. Whatever you dwell upon, you attract into your life. So if you think doom and gloom, that's what you'll get. Think happiness and optimism, and they're already yours. In Chapter 4 we said that your unconscious attitudes determine your situation. But where do all your unconscious attitudes come from? They are created by your own thoughts, fed in by your conscious mind. So negative people constantly create problems and misery for themselves; conversely, positive people attract good fortune, success and happiness. Why?

The answer lies in the Law of Cause and Effect. This law states that there is no such thing as an accident and nothing ever happens without a reason. Think about it. Striking a drum causes a sound to be made. Watering a plant helps it to grow. The creation of an artistic masterpiece, the building of a skyscraper, even flying to the moon – nothing ever happens without cause. The law is universal and, like gravity, it makes no difference whether you believe in it or not. Its force will still pull you to the ground.

The ancestor of every action is a thought.

Ralph Waldo Emerson

Now reflect for a moment. What do striking a drum, watering a plant and building a skyscraper have in common? Each is 'caused' by a single, human thought. 'I think I'll hit that drum.' 'The plants need watering.' 'I need more office space.' Can you think of any action that didn't ultimately begin with a thought? You can't. It's impossible.

You can't scratch your head, blow your nose, tie your shoelaces or, in fact, do anything without first thinking about it, even if it's only for a fraction of a second. In fact, your every thought has had an effect on this very moment. You are the sum total of all the thoughts you have ever had. Yes, your past thoughts, like a row of dominoes each pushing over the next, have brought you to this point in your life. As an ancient Chinese proverb puts it:

Sow a thought, reap an action.
Sow an action, reap a habit.
Sow a habit, reap a character.
Sow a character, reap a destiny.

In other words, your overall destiny is shaped by your thoughts. If you don't control them, they'll control you: just as inevitably as if you were to let go of the steering wheel of a car.

We know dozens of positive, optimistic people whose lives

are enjoyable and fulfilling, but since there isn't space for them all we'd like to tell you about a 78-year-old bundle of joy called Peggy who first approached Rex for help with a minor back problem. One day when she was watching the weather forecast, the presenter remarked that: 'It's going to be a terribly miserable rainy day.' It was probably the last time he ever said that, for Peggy immediately took up pen and paper and wrote to the BBC. She pointed out that 'there is nothing miserable about rain, which gives us our lovely green countryside, and many viewers might have become needlessly depressed by the picture painted by such an unfortunate choice of words'. Peggy still treasures the letter she received in reply, thanking her and promising not to use such negative phrasing again.

Cheerfulness and positivity came as naturally to Peggy as breathing the fresh country air of her childhood home, but she took no credit for it. She said she'd always been lucky. Right from the start, she'd had one big advantage – her Dad. Peggy remembered him as a wise, gentle, encouraging and unfailingly optimistic man. He was her constant source of inspiration, and the role model for her own positive thinking.

'I'm really a lazy person,' says Peggy, 'and I just can't be bothered to go to the trouble of thinking negatively. It's so much easier to be positive.' In truth, Peggy is not at all lazy. First thing every morning throughout the year she goes for a swim in the sea near her home. She's even appeared on television, shown breaking through a layer of ice early one freezing January morning in order to take her dip.

Peggy's faced many trying times and many disappointments and come through them a stronger and wiser person. She views all setbacks as opportunities to learn and she always searches for a positive meaning. A few years ago, she twice failed an exam which would have qualified her as a radio ham. Did she give up? Not a bit of it. She thought of all the wonderful people she'd meet by reattending the classes and trying again. She eventually became the oldest person ever to pass the exam.

The inspirational Peggy transforms the lives of the people

with whom she comes into contact with her infectious smile and positivity. She's now completely healthy, but still visits Rex regularly. 'Because I enjoy the chat,' she says. But Rex suspects that he learns more from her than she does from him.

Peggy is a perfect example of how early positive conditioning and constructive thinking can stand you in good stead for the rest of your life, but sadly we find many examples at the other end of the spectrum. Why are there so many negative people in the world and so few Peggys? For some reason, most people find it much easier to hold on to negative thoughts than positive ones. On average a person can only hold a positive thought for 4–7 seconds whereas they can worry for hours, days or even years about something that hasn't yet occurred.

Possibly, many people simply don't understand the relationship between their thoughts and the universal forces that can support or destroy you, frustrate you or help you to succeed. This has been demonstrated many times in the arts, sport, relationships and so on, even business. For instance, an American finance company conducted a study on experienced sales representatives. They found that positive thinkers had sales 37 percent above the average. It revolutionized their recruitment methods. Dispensing with entrance exams, they recruited a hundred new staff who scored high on optimism. Before long, they were selling 10 percent more than average. Why?

Let's look again at the Law of Cause and Effect, but from a slightly different angle. Your thoughts are like voices chattering away inside your head. You talk to yourself incessantly, at a rate of about six hundred words per minute. You are constantly questioning, judging, criticizing and sometimes condemning yourself. Listen carefully to these voices. Do they form a pattern?

We think they do. It's like having two characters in your head: a 'Thinker' and a 'Prover'. The Thinker, located in your conscious mind, puts forward a proposition: 'Life's rotten. Bad things always happen to me.' The Prover, housed in the unconscious, dutifully takes it upon itself to marshall the evidence. It scours your memory banks for anything that 'proves' how awful life has been for you. Rest assured, proof will be found, because that's the way it's made.

> *My life has been filled with the most dreadful*
> *misfortune, most of which never happened.*

Michel Eyquem Montagne

Now back to those insurance sales representatives. Let's say John is downhearted. His career is failing and he's in danger of losing his job. 'I'm useless,' he tells himself. 'I haven't a hope. It's all too difficult for me. I might as well give up. I just don't get the breaks.' How will the Prover relate to these instructions?

In the next office sits Fiona, a keen new recruit. She hasn't done well either. 'It's early days, and I'm improving every day. I'm sure if I keep trying I'll succeed. Every day my enthusiasm strengthens as my experience grows.'

Who's more likely to succeed?

The Thinker and the Prover: the law of cause and effect. Both demonstrate how your thoughts influence your actions, which determine the results you get. *You take control of your life by taking control of your thinking.* Practising the techniques in the next few chapters will help you control your thinking.

> *Unless there be correct thought, there cannot be*
> *any action, and when there is correct thought,*
> *right action will follow.*

Henry George

So what path are your thoughts leading you down? If you don't relish the journey, it is time to change direction.

'But surely,' you might say, 'I can't change my thoughts.

They just appear. They float in and out of my head of their own volition. I can't do anything to stop them.'

If you're determined to cling to this view, you're deluding yourself. It simply isn't true. Yes, thousands of thoughts float into your mind every day, most of them quite innocuous, but you always have the choice: to hold on to them, or release them. If you don't want a particular thought, you can consciously and deliberately discard it. If it's a negative thought, the sooner the better, otherwise it will seep through into your unconscious and keep coming back to haunt you.

So remember, whatever you sow, you reap. Thoughts are causes, actions are effects. Constructive thoughts lead to constructive action. Destructive thoughts lead to destructive actions. Are you getting the results you want in your life, yes or no? If the answer is no, examine your thoughts.

Thoughts are powerful entities that have tremendous energy. Realize that *improving the quality of your thoughts improves the quality of your life*. The next two chapters tell you how you can achieve this in a simple, four-step process:

- Practise mindfulness and awareness
- Get rid of negative thoughts
- Feed in the positives
- Enjoy the results.

Now read on.

9 Eradicating Negative Thoughts

Thinking is like living and dying.
Each of us must do it for himself.

Josiah Royce

A student who had completed his studies with the master went to thank him and ask for some last words of wisdom to send him on his way. However, it was the master's day of silence, so he gestured for a piece of paper and a pen and wrote down one word, 'Awareness'. The student was puzzled and asked him to explain. The mater wrote, 'Awareness, awareness, awareness'. That didn't help either, so the student asked for a fuller explanation. This time the master wrote, 'Awareness, awareness, awareness means awareness'.

In other words, awareness is the key to everything: awareness of what's happening around you and within you. You should develop the ability to be 'aware' of your surroundings, people's thoughts and feelings, and their reactions to you. You also need to be conscious of what's happening inside you, of your *own* thoughts, feelings and reactions. We call the practice of mentally stepping back – directing your mind inwards and observing your thoughts – 'mindfulness'.

You can experience mindfulness wherever and whenever you choose. You certainly don't have to restrict it to a special time or place: it is simply a matter of getting into the habit of noting your thoughts and reactions to everything you do. The great advantage of developing this ability is this: it will help you to quieten your left brain and bring your right brain to the fore, heightening your intuitive and creative powers.

Now you've got used to the idea that thoughts are things that shape events, you'll understand how important it is to take charge of them. *Developing mindfulness is the first step.*

From **self-awareness**
  comes **self-knowledge**
    which leads to **insight**
      From **insight**
        comes **practical wisdom**
          which leads to
            the **awakening of real intelligence**
            and **effective action.**

Bear in mind that self-awareness is especially powerful when you are in Alpha level. Perhaps you are sceptical of the idea that you're *more* aware when you're in this quiet, dreamy state. If so, next time you relax note how little sounds around you seem louder. A quietly ticking alarm clock sounds quite loud; the noise of the traffic outside seems to reverberate. Then passively observe your own thoughts. You can simply watch them floating in and out of your head. Don't be self-critical or judgemental, just pay attention and take note. Isolate any destructive and negative words and phrases and gently rectify any that are not contributing to your wellbeing. The more you practise, the more your insight and self-understanding will grow.

What's happening when you focus your attention inwardly in this way? Well, you've discovered another way of looking at your mind, another plane of understanding. We've already said a lot about the mind, but now we're going to examine it in a slightly different way.

The Conditioned and Reflective Minds

Let's take another look at your analytical left brain. Obviously, it's essential for coping with day-to-day activities but, unfortunately, it has a fundamental drawback. It relies solely on past experiences for its information and, as a direct result, *it gets things wrong*. It links pleasure and pain to everything that happened. It 'assumes' that they will be experienced all over again if the same behaviour is repeated. That is why *it makes mistakes*.

Relying too heavily on the left brain, or 'conditioned mind', leads to your thoughts and actions becoming nothing more than reflex-like reactions to your memories. No wonder it can be a liability. It's obvious that you cannot always rely on past experiences for coping with today's reality; doing this will lead to great disappointment, as our friend John Jordan discovered.

In 1972 he was invited to invest £100 in a new business selling computer equipment. Hoping to make a quick return, he borrowed the money and bought some shares. Within a year, the company folded and he lost his investment. Nearly 20 years later, John, by now a computer systems analyst, was given the opportunity to invest £5,000 in a new venture producing and selling computer games. Initially, he was very attracted to the idea. Then doubts started to surface. 'Last time I invested money in a new business', he told his friend, Paul, 'I lost the lot. I don't want to get caught out again. It's too big a risk.' He turned the opportunity down, but Paul decided that he wanted to invest. Two years later, Paul came up trumps. The business was such a tremendous success that it had already made its investors a three-fold return.

This course of events shows you why you can't always rely on your old memories to guide you in the present. The past most definitely does not equate with the future. But, fortunately, there is a another part of the mind that does not rely on material from the past. We call it the 'reflective mind'. It is housed in the unconscious and can be accessed via the right brain. The reflective mind can perceive the link between cause and effect, without judging, criticizing or condemning. It has the ability to pinpoint precisely where the conditioned mind is going wrong, and correct it.

You may be wondering how you can you use this powerful

reflective mind, but you actually already know the answer. You do it by dropping into Alpha level and quietening the conditioned mind. This done, you use your heightened state of mindfulness to observe where your thoughts are leading you. Then, if it proves necessary, simply change them.

For example, Terry was a 40-year-old who'd been mistreated by his father as a child. His outlook on life had been subsequently scarred. He thought he understood why after a therapist had convinced him that his father was the cause. He was told his mind would be forever damaged by these events and there was nothing he could do about it. However, by learning to go into Alpha, he understood clearly that what happened 30-odd years ago need no longer have any effect on the present. With help, he learned to eliminate harmful thoughts and replace them with new, constructive ones. After being taught to use his reflective mind to observe, it gradually dawned on him: he had been shackled by his conditioning. Aided by this insight, he reprogrammed his conditioned mind. It took some months of patient practice, but once he'd mastered it, he was able to attain new heights of happiness and success.

Terry had correctly mastered the art of gaining the insight he needed from his reflective mind and then using this in conjunction with his conditioned mind to correct his unhappy situation. This is the right procedure. Always use the facilities of your left brain *after* you have sought insight from the right. *Not before*, or you will be relying on the redundant tapes of your past.

How to Get Rid of Negative Thoughts

The technique for eradicating unwanted thoughts is called 'conscious thought stopping' and it's so straightforward you may even think it simplistic. It consists of stopping negative thoughts dead in their tracks before they can cause permanent damage. It works like this.

As soon as you become aware of a negative thought, break

the pattern and exorcize it. Say 'Stop! Go away! Cancel!' and do something physical, like clapping your hands (the sound will help to interrupt your negative pattern). If you are in company and don't want to draw attention to yourself, try pinching yourself on the arm. You can also imagine closing a book, a symbolic gesture that that's the end of it. Now, immediately replace the harmful thought with an empowering one.

If you catch yourself thinking negatively, don't be angry or frustrated. The more you chastise yourself, the more incompetent you'll feel and the more slip-ups you'll make. This downward spiral can continue indefinitely. Far better to just change the thought and congratulate yourself on your progress. Look at the situation positively and say: 'I've been doing very well, so one small slip won't bother me.' You will then feel much better about yourself, making it less likely that you'll repeat the mistake.

To speed up your progress, you can step up a gear and put yourself on a 'mental diet'.

The Seven-day Mental Diet

The Seven-day Mental Diet was invented by Emmett Fox in the 1930s and is as effective at clearing out your mental cobwebs as a raw juice diet is at cleaning out your digestive system. Begin when you're reasonably certain the time is right, for you must feel committed to seeing it through. All you have to do then is follow these three simple rules.

Rule 1

For seven consecutive days, release any negative thoughts or feelings. Veto unhelpful words and phrases, and refuse to dwell on problems or defeats. Tell yourself you are not going to allow yourself to worry about anything for more than 60 seconds at a time before dismissing it from your mind.

Rule 2

If you should find yourself taken unawares by a negative thought or feeling, instantly use thought stopping to cancel it, then immediately replace it with either the opposite or another suitable positive word or phrase.

Rule 3

If you backslide, don't get annoyed with yourself. A negative thought won't cause you any harm if you deal with it immediately. But if you continue to focus on it for, say, 60 seconds or more, you must wait until the following morning and start all over again. Go back to day one and keep counting until the seven days are up.

Having managed it once, why not try it for another week, and then another, until you've managed it for a whole month? Once you've completed the Seven-day Mental Diet, you'll find you've ingrained a healthy new thinking pattern into your consciousness. It will be easy for you to keep a constant check on your level of positivity. You can ask yourself, 'On a scale of one to ten, how positive am I being today?' If it's less than seven or eight, then you'd better try a little harder. Nine or ten, and you deserve to be congratulated.

Once you've completed your seven-day mental diet, you'll find that thought stopping becomes instinctive. Warning bells sound as your automatic 'negative thinking' alarm swings into action. Eventually this will become totally unnecessary, because once unwelcome thoughts realize they'll be firmly dealt with they won't even bother trying to enter your head.

Crash! One of your best china dinner plates slips out of your hand and smashes on to the floor. Your (untrained) inner voice demands to know why you are so clumsy. Another voice replies that you can't help it, clumsiness is part of your make-up. 'You're careless and stupid', it adds, probably sounding remarkably like one of your parents. Your memory responds by replaying past incidents when you broke things: your brother's favourite toy (you were given a good ticking off for that, weren't you?); Grandma's best vase (wasn't she furious!) and that expensive crystal glass that slipped out of your hand at your parents' silver wedding anniversary.

You'll recognize the Thinker and the Prover at work again. Before long, the Prover has successfully convinced you that you're not only careless and clumsy, but muddle-headed, thick-skulled and worthless as well. All because of a minor accident!

But, remember, that was before you learned thought stopping and went on the Seven-day Mental Diet. Now you know exactly how to eradicate negative thoughts. You understand the importance of this. You are aware that they block your connection to your inner wisdom and the Universal Intelligence – the Source of all knowledge. You won't allow them to hold back your progress either materially or spiritually any longer. Now you're ready to move on to the next step – feeding in the positives.

10 Feeding in the Positives

*If you keep saying things are going to be bad
you have a good chance of being a prophet.*

Isaac Bashevis Singer

'I just wasn't thinking.' How often have you used this
line when you've slipped up? Strictly speaking though, this
is not possible. You are always thinking, consciously or
unconsciously. You can't *not* think. It could be positive
or negative, but never both. You cannot be aware of more
than one thought at a time, so when you clear out your
old thinking patterns, you must replace them instantly with
plenty of positive material – before the old ones return to
haunt you.

Cast your mind back to the plate-breaking incident at the
end of the last chapter. Now imagine the scene again, but this
time, instead of berating yourself, say 'Stop!', clap your hands
together sharply and tell yourself, 'Cancel that thought! I'm
not stupid. I am a strong and worthy person. It was only an
accident. Accidents can happen to anyone, it's no big deal.
The plate can easily be replaced.' Now you are feeding your
unconscious a very different set of instructions. The 'Prover'
will search your memory banks and find plenty of evidence
that you're okay. 'It must be ages since I last broke anything.
I'm very careful. I look after my things well, and they usually
last for years!' Now, your mind is reinforcing your positive
self-image, absolving you from guilt and suggesting a different
attitude. You'll soon be able to forget about the incident
altogether.

Let's take another example. You're resitting an examination. Once upon a time you would have told yourself: 'I

failed it last time because I was so nervous, even though I knew my stuff. No doubt I'll fail it again, because my nerves are bound to get the better of me.' Your 'Prover' would have bombarded you with a barrage of so-called evidence. 'Yes, that's me all over, like when I took my driving test and I went totally blank when I saw the pictures of road signs. And when I sat my exams, I completely messed up that question about the sex life of barnacles. I'm useless at exams.' Before you knew it, you were rigid with fear at the prospect of repeating the whole fiasco, all because you once had a few butterflies in your stomach, as everyone does. And this might not even have been the reason you failed – perhaps you didn't revise thoroughly enough or were unlucky with the questions.

But that was the *old* you, before you learned how to drop the destructive thoughts. The question now arises, 'What should I replace them with?'

Positive Self-talk

Plato once remarked that when the mind is thinking, it is talking to itself. We call this inner conversation the 'internal dialogue', and by now we don't have to remind you how important it is. With your developing mindfulness, you're becoming more and more aware of what you say when you talk to yourself and, hopefully, determined to take charge.

Negative self-talk brings misery, ill-health and worry. It saps your energy, kills your enthusiasm, dampens your spirits and weakens your inner power. Your Higher Self certainly doesn't want to listen to it, and knows how difficult it is to shout over it, so it stops trying and retreats quietly into the background. When this happens, you're out of tune with the flow of life altogether. You've cut yourself off from the Source.

On the other hand, positive self-talk is perhaps the most effective way of overriding your negative conditioning, providing you keep at it. It transforms your mood, strengthens your resolve and fills you with energy and zest for life. So here's a new maxim we strongly encourage you to adopt:

Never say anything, either to yourself or to anyone else, silently or out loud, that you don't sincerely want to be true.

Here are some common examples of disempowering self-talk*:

> 'I can't . . .'
> 'It's impossible.'
> 'I'm useless at . . .'
> 'Everybody's against me.'
> 'Nothing ever works out the way I want it to.'

This kind of self-talk cripples you. It's like trying to play the piano with both hands tied behind your back. Parents often tell their children there's no such word as 'can't' – if only it were true. *Eliminate the 'I can'ts' from this moment on* and you'll have destroyed the most insidious of all your enemies.

Now let's look at:

> 'I'll try to . . .'
> 'I ought to . . .'
> 'I wish I could . . .'

What's coming next? Usually a silent 'but' followed by 'I can't'. 'I'll try to do better (but I don't think I can)'. 'I ought to work harder (but I don't expect I will)'. 'I wish I could

---

* We recommend Shad Helmstetter's book, *What To Say When You Talk To Yourself*, and are indebted to him for some of these examples.

live in a warm country (but I know I can't)'. These kind of phrases have a built-in sting in the tail. They imply failure. Once again, they are best avoided altogether, so instead of: 'I'll try to make it to the meeting on Wednesday', say 'I will (or I will not) attend'. How about:

> 'I used to . . .'
> 'I no longer . . .'
> 'I never . . .'

Here, you are stating a firm resolve to change and instructing your unconscious to help you. But it's important to remember that the physical change doesn't *need* to have taken place before you adopt this pattern of self-talk. You might hear a little voice piping up, 'Don't be silly, of course you do, who are you trying to kid?' This is just your conditioned mind attempting to hang on to old habits. Suspend disbelief for a while, safe in the knowledge that your deeds will soon catch up with your words. For example, a compulsive nailbiter starts telling herself, 'I never bite my nails. I used to bite them, but now I don't.' For a while, she may continue to bite her nails, but every time she does, she'll become more and more aware of it. 'What are you doing with your fingers in your mouth?' asks the Thinker. 'You no longer bite your nails.' Before long, the Prover has reprogrammed her unconscious habit patterns and the nailbiting stops.

Now consider:

> 'I can . . .'
> 'I am . . .'
> 'I do . . .'
> 'I have . . .'

Complete these sentences as you wish, for example: 'I *am* a confident and capable person!' 'I *can* succeed at whatever I choose!' 'I *have* a well-paid and enjoyable job!'

There's plenty of punch behind these affirmations, the most positive self-talk of all. You're affirming that this is the way you want to be, and passing the instruction to your unconscious to 'get to it'. You're starting to create your dreams and bring them into reality. Gone are the words of lack and limitation, the doubts and uncertainties. Instead, feelings of pleasure and power take their place. 'I like myself!' 'I love everybody, and everybody loves me!' 'I am determined, enthusiastic, powerful!' We challenge you to say any of these phrases a few times as if you really mean it and not feel different. Try it: you'll discover it really works.

Wordpower

Wordpower is an extension of positive self-talk. Words have a definite effect on your mood. Tell yourself you feel 'depressed' and it's hard not to feel miserable. Try it for yourself. Now say 'I feel terrific', as if you really mean it, and try *not* to feel enthusiastic and invigorated. Almost impossible!

'But words are only labels,' you might say. 'They describe how I am feeling, but they are not the feeling itself.' This is true, but it's a two-way effect. Your words not only reflect your experiences, but also your reactions to them. Remember Dynamic Living Principle number 1: 'You create your own reality with your thoughts, feelings and attitudes.' Change the words and you modify the impact events have on you. For instance, you can use words to take the edge off a bad feeling, or make a good feeling even better.

Dave once helped a young client suffering from depression. He encouraged her to stop telling herself she was 'depressed', but to say she was feeling 'a little low' instead. Within a few days, this simple change had already made her feel very much better. So next time you are feeling 'angry', 'guilty' or 'worried', try changing the words to 'a bit upset', 'regretful' or 'a touch concerned'. It will soften the impact of the negative feeling.

Equally, next time you feel 'happy' or 'confident' or 'determined', try using words that reinforce these already good feelings. How about 'ecstatic', 'unbeatable' or 'unstoppable'?

Notice what happens: the chances are you'll feel more alive, more alert and full of energy.

Perhaps your parents were right after all. From now on there is no such word as 'can't': eliminate it from your vocabulary! Then scrap words and phrases which suggest doubt, inadequacy, hopelessness, failure or laziness. Be on your guard against 'should' or 'shouldn't', which normally signal your old conditioning rearing its ugly head once more. If someone asks 'How are you?' don't answer, 'Not too bad' or 'Mustn't grumble', which don't inspire any great enthusiasm; instead say 'Great! Couldn't be better!' Everybody has their own favourite words and phrases, so the best approach is to be mindful of the language you use and experiment a bit. Which words make you feel good? Which substitutions work for you?

Start by changing intensely negative words to gentler ones and mild positives to strong positives. Then mild negatives to mild positives. Then when you get really good at it, you'll be able to jump straight from negative words to positive ones and alter your mood at will. Never miss an opportunity; you'll soon notice the difference.

Every time you feed in positive thoughts, you alter the balance of the contents of your mental bucket. It's like dripping white paint into a tin of black. At first it makes hardly any difference, but after a while the colour starts to change from black to dark grey, then light grey and eventually white.

One of Rex's patients, John, had had a difficult life and a particularly tough childhood. Rex taught him some relaxation exercises (which he practised regularly) and the positive thinking techniques you've just been reading about. After six weeks, John was rather disappointed as nothing seemed to be happening.

'But John, you're 38 years old,' Rex pointed out, and explained the analogy of the black and white paint. 'You've had more than two hundred thousand negative thoughts throughout your life. Only in the last few weeks have you begun to think positively. That makes four or five hundred positive thoughts. It's going to take a few more to really make an impact. You have to keep going.' John certainly did, and after a while happily reported that he'd made some positive decisions and things were definitely looking up.

Much of our self-talk is like a quiz: a series of questions and answers. Let's have a closer look.

Positive Questions

Your internal dialogue can turn into a seemingly endless interrogation of your obedient servant, the Prover. It is programmed to come up with an answer to anything you ask, even if the question is totally groundless or irrelevant. If you ask, 'Why am I so stupid?' it will provide you with an answer, even if you're not stupid at all. Remember, the 'Prover' can't think for itself. It has no way of knowing whether the basis of your question is valid; it will go ahead and search your unconscious data banks anyway. So a question like, 'Why do I *always* get it wrong?' will be answered even if you only *occasionally* make mistakes.

Far better to ask yourself an empowering question, such as 'How can I handle this situation?' 'What can I learn from this?' 'What do I need to do to get the result I want?' Have you spotted the difference? Now the 'Prover' assumes that you want a solution to your problem and takes it as an instruction to find one. Positive questions can change your mood very quickly and put you in the right frame of mind to deal with any situation.

Keep at it and Enjoy the Results

Rex once told a patient called Ellen of an incident from his college days. The lecturer came in one morning carrying half a bottle of milk. He placed it on the table in front of him and 'accidentally' knocked it over. Without making a fuss, he produced a cloth and calmly wiped it up. 'What's the moral of this?' he asked the class. 'It's no use crying over spilt milk,' came the reply.

This story made quite an impact on Ellen, who had been suffering from stress symptoms and quite often lost her cool over quite trivial incidents. A few days later, minutes before some important dinner guests were due to arrive, she accidentally knocked a pot plant off the window sill all over the main course, smothering it in a soggy mess of black compost. For a few seconds, panic threatened to overwhelm her.

'The first thing that came into my head was, "Oh no, why am I so stupid?" I knew my husband would start shouting if he saw what I'd done,' she said, 'and I could feel the frustration welling up inside me. And then suddenly I remembered what you'd said about not crying over spilt milk. I took a deep breath, told myself I couldn't undo what had been done, and asked, "Right, what do I need to do to keep calm and get back on track?" The answer came quickly. "Take charge of your thoughts." "Right," I told myself, "I can handle this easily. I am cool and calm." I wiped up the mess and, luckily, had something in the freezer which I defrosted in the microwave. My husband and his friends didn't even realize what had happened!'

A few days later, Ellen's resolve was tested again. The washing machine sprung a leak and flooded the kitchen with several inches of soapy water. 'I didn't get stressed at all,' she said proudly. 'I resisted an impulse to scream, kicked off my shoes and started mopping up. When I'd finished, I sat down, had a cup of tea, and congratulated myself. A few months earlier I would have gone beserk. What a difference!' The trick is to be on your guard and control any angry thoughts at the outset.

Like Ellen, you'll have to be vigilant. Whether you like it or not, you are surrounded by people who take pleasure in an 'Isn't it awful' mentality, which constantly feeds on itself. Look at the reaction to BBC newsreader Martyn Lewis' impassioned plea for more good news on television, in the spring of 1993. 'Try to sell any TV news editor a story of success or achievement,' he said. 'Unless it is a 'slow' news day, reactions range from 'Sorry, no room' to 'not a puff for that'. We consign viewers to growing up in a relentless culture of negativity – of naturally expecting things to go wrong, and finding it ever harder to believe that anything in life is achievable.'

Fellow journalists reacted with contempt. 'He wants to sanitize the news,' said one. The fact is, good news doesn't sell newspapers, and what sells newspapers reflects the national mood.

Experiments have shown that, although you can remove someone from their normal environment and successfully teach them to think and act positively, they will often revert to their old ways when they return to their regular circle. You can't change your family, friends and workmates overnight, so how are you going to make sure they don't drag you down? Here are some suggestions.

- Enlist their support. Tell them what you are trying to achieve. Ask them to point out gently when they think you're slipping.
- If certain individuals are doggedly negative, minimize your contact with them or avoid them altogether until your new positive approach has become part of you.
- Avoid newspapers and news broadcasts first thing in the morning and last thing at night, when your unconscious mind is most receptive. If you want to keep abreast of the news, be aware of the negative slant and don't allow it to affect you.
- Give yourself rewards for your progress. At the end of each successful day, congratulate yourself or allow yourself a treat. Anticipating a little self-indulgence reinforces your determination and encourages you to keep going.
- If you are facing a difficult situation, spend most of your time focusing on the solution, not the problem. Ask yourself positive questions such as 'How can I overcome this?' or 'What else can I do that I haven't already thought of?'

- Look for the good in any situation – there is *always some*. For example, Peggy's (remember her?) cat died a few months ago and, although for a short while she felt devastated, she was soon able to think back on all the pleasure it had given her.

Positive thought puts you in touch with the life force and brings out the power within, so now *apply* what you've read and you will begin to transform your life. They say 'Knowledge is power', but that's not strictly true. Knowledge is *potential* power, but it is less than useless unless you do something with it. Otherwise, you might as well try to cure your next cold by reading the ingredients on a medicine bottle! So get going right away. This very minute. Don't be put off if things don't go according to plan or you find yourself slipping. It's no disgrace and it's certainly not defeat, because defeat is simply the decision to give up.

Decide that from this moment on you're going to take charge of your thoughts, and keep at it. Then you can't fail.

11 Affirmations

TRANSFORM YOUR CONSCIOUS MIND WITH THE DYNAMIC LIVING
PRINCIPLES AND YOUR UNCONSCIOUS WITH THE DYNAMIC
LIVING FORMULA.

Dynamic Living Principle 9

Positive self-talk is a big step forward, but you can increase
its power and persuasiveness by backing it up with a carefully
planned programme of affirmations. An affirmation is defined
in the dictionary as a solemn declaration of the truth of
something. One of the best known was formulated by Emil
Coué in the 1920s: 'Every day in every way, I'm getting
better and better.' Many people have improved their health
dramatically by habitually repeating that one famous phrase.
Some examples of affirmations were given in the last chapter.
Another is the old Sunday School song:

> *I'm H A P P Y*
> *I'm H A P P Y*
> *I know I am, I'm sure I am,*
> *I'm H A P P Y.*

It's almost impossible to feel anything other than happy
after a few rousing choruses. What you are really doing
is tuning into the enormous power of suggestion. This can
be used for good or evil. An African witch doctor, for
example, can cause a member of the tribe to die instantly
by merely pointing an animal bone at him and 'casting a
spell'. The very suggestion, coupled with the victim's implicit

belief that the witch doctor has this power, is enough to kill him.

Doctors have found that pills and potions with no active ingredients (placebos) can cure illness because the patient *believes* that they will do the trick. Dave once had a client who wanted help with a fear of flying. At one time, this had been alleviated by pills prescribed by his doctor which had made him feel sleepy during the flight, but over time the effects had worn off. He had mentioned this to the doctor, who told him that he wasn't altogether surprised because there were no active ingredients in the tablets anyway. With this knowledge, the symptoms had returned with a vengeance, worse than ever before.

You've probably benefited from suggestion many times in your life; for instance, when you fell over and hurt your knee as a child, did your Mum or Dad ever 'kiss it better'? It did feel better, of course, even though there is no 'logical' explanation why it should. So you know suggestion works; why not make full use of it – in this case, self-suggestion using affirmations.

You can devise a programme of affirmations to help you achieve what you want. A friend of ours, Marie, firmly believes in their power. She sets aside an hour every evening to go through hers. Recently she was working as a freelance writer and visualizing and affirming that she would soon have a word processor. After two months, an editor rang up out of the blue and asked what she was using for her work. When she told him it was a rather battered old typewriter, he immediately offered her the use of a word processor (the exact model she had affirmed) and promised to have it delivered later that morning.

But this wasn't the end of it. She didn't yet have a printer, so she started visualizing and affirming that one would materialize. Two weeks later, a friend mentioned that he had one in his attic that she could have if it was compatible with her machine, and fortunately it was.

The proprietor of a top school for fashion models was once asked how she managed to turn out such stunning girls. She invited the enquirer to see for himself. It turned out that the girls spent the first week of their training walking up and down in front of large mirrors with books balanced on their heads declaring aloud, 'I am beautiful, I am beautiful', over and over again. By the end of the first week, the change was dramatic; their posture and facial expression had changed and their confidence had blossomed. They were radiating an aura of beauty simply because they had come to believe they were beautiful.

You can bring about similar changes in yourself: look in the mirror. Tell yourself, 'I am beautiful', 'I am a strong and worthy person', or, perhaps the most powerful affirmation of all, 'I like myself'. How do you feel?

Looking in the mirror as you recite your affirmations increases their effectiveness, but there are other methods as well. For instance, list them on cards which you can carry around and read throughout the day. Stick them to your bathroom mirror, steering wheel or fridge, anywhere you routinely look. Record them on to cassette tape and listen frequently. Jot them down in your diary and chequebook. If your goal is a physical acquisition, carry a photograph of it around with you and affirm that it is yours. Write your affirmations out every day – the act of writing reinforces them in your unconscious.

Although you can recite your affirmations at any time, they are most likely to hit home when you are relaxed. Otherwise, your conscious mind will sit up and voice its objections: 'Don't be so silly, of course you're not beautiful, you can't fool me!' 'You've never had confidence before, so what makes you think you'll get it now?' Affirming when in Alpha is called 'autosuggestion'. It's especially effective because your unconscious is more receptive then to your positive suggestions.

Using Affirmations

Affirmations can be used for many purposes.

- **To support and facilitate achievement of your goals.**
  'I shall persist until I succeed.'
  'Every day, I get closer and closer to achieving my goal.'

- **To replace negative attitudes from the past.**
  'I now release with ease all old negative beliefs.'
  'I am responsible for my own feelings.'

- **To build into yourself the qualities you need.**
  'I am determined, patient and courageous.'
  'I am getting more and more enthusiastic about . . .'

- **To foster positive mental attitudes.**
  'I take responsibility for the quality of my life.'
  'I think, talk and act positively at all times.'

- **To build self-confidence and self-belief.**
  'I accept, love and approve of myself.'
  'I respect and admire myself.'
  'I believe in myself.'

- **To relax and combat stress.**
  'I am cool and calm, peaceful and relaxed at all times.'
  'I can relax and free myself of stress. Peace and tranquillity fill my heart.'

- **To help you cultivate fulfilling relationships with yourself and others.**
  'I am a good, loyal, dependable friend.'
  'I am open and accepting of myself and others.'
  'I am loving, lovable and loved.'

The Five Ps

*Language is the picture and
counterpart of thought.*

Mark Hopkins

By now you're probably dying to get started with your own affirmations, but be careful. There are certain rules you must observe, otherwise they may backfire. We call them the 'Five Ps'. You'll notice that they apply equally to other forms of self-talk and, as you'll discover in the next two chapters, to creative imagery.

1 Personalize

You cannot make affirmations on behalf of other people, so always make them personal. One way to ensure you observe this rule is to start every affirmation with 'I'.

There is, however, one exception to this rule, and that is when using the 'first, second and third person' technique, a very powerful routine for strengthening your affirmations. Let's suppose you are improving your self-confidence using the affirmation, 'I am a confident person'. Add your first name and recite it as follows:

> 'I, Chris, am a confident person.
> You, Chris, are a confident person.
> Chris is a confident person.'

All three affirmations still refer to you and no one else; all you've done is reinforce them by changing your use of language.

2 Present Tense

Always state your affirmations in the present. If you were to use the future tense, your unconscious would assume that it can postpone what you want because it isn't a priority. If it's a physical object, see it as already yours, belonging to you and in your possession. Say, 'I own' rather than 'I will own'. If you want to make some change to yourself, such as losing weight or becoming more courageous, say, 'I am slim' rather than 'I will be slim', or 'I am brave' not 'I will be brave'.

It is usually necessary to suspend disbelief, especially if you are working on acquiring an item that you clearly don't yet have – but don't let this bother you. Although you may feel you're lying to yourself, remember that you are in the early stages of creating something which will eventually materialize. When you say 'I have a widget', what you really mean is that it is already there in essence, and soon it will be there in reality!

The Hopi Indians of North America are able to manifest seemingly impossible things like rain, but they say there is nothing magical about it. 'White man' apparently had the same abilities a long time ago but has forgotten how to use them. Using an affirmation is rather like planting a seed. Be patient, and it will grow and flower.

3 Positive

Many years ago, it was discovered that the unconscious mind is incapable of distinguishing a negative word, and often overlooks one if it occurs in the middle of a sentence. So, for example, if you were to say 'I can *not* fail', the word 'fail' will register. It is far better to say, 'I can succeed'. Similarly, 'I am now a positive thinker' will get much better results than 'I'm not going to think negative thoughts anymore', and 'I am slim' is better than 'I'm not fat'.

It's best to avoid all negative words and phrases wherever possible, because they confuse and you might inadvertently end up with the opposite to that which you intended.

4 Power

When you're reciting an affirmation, say it as if you really mean it. The greater the emotional power you can muster, the better, because emotion provides the energy which brings your wishes into reality. Imagine the sense of pleasure you would feel; try to taste the fruits of your efforts in advance. Use a persuasive tone of voice; speak with conviction; picture your dreams coming true, exactly as you envisaged.

A weak and weedy voice would probably be ignored by other people, so why assume your unconscious is any different?

5 Practise

Practice makes permanent, so recite your affirmations constantly, wherever you are. As we've said, only application will bring about the changes you desire. Remember, you can have anything you want provided you put in the necessary time, energy and practice. Last thing at night is a good time, because your mind is at its most receptive and will have something uplifting to work on while you are asleep. Remember, it only takes 28 days to change a habit, so keep at it.

> Destiny is not a matter of chance, it is a
> matter of choice; it is not a thing to be
> waited for, it is a thing to be achieved.
>
> William Jennings Bryan

The Firewalk

Imagine the scene: an English meadow on a cold, wet spring evening. About 40 rather anxious people from all walks of life, including Rex and Dave, barefoot, circling a 13 foot lane of burning hot coals. At one end, the 'gatekeepers', there to encourage and support; at the other, a bucket of ice-cold water. One by one, the participants step tentatively on to the coals, muttering 'cool, wet moss' under their breath, then, relieved that they feel no pain, walk all the way across and douse their feet in the water.

What's the secret? Voodoo? Trickery? Not at all! The firewalk is a convincing demonstration of mind over matter, proof that we are all capable of transcending our physical bodies. Science cannot explain how it is possible, but it is. We've seen it and done it for ourselves. Firewalking is nothing new, of course. It was a common form of initiation all over the ancient world, and thousands of people have accomplished it in Britain, Continental Europe, America and elsewhere in recent years.

How *did* we do it? Primarily by drawing on the techniques we've described in the last few chapters, because self-talk played a big part. As a group, we'd chanted and recited affirmations such as 'I am cool and calm', 'I walk through fear' and 'I am powerful'. When the time came to walk on fire, we were mentally prepared and in a positive emotional state. The burning coals genuinely felt like crunchy, cold popcorn. When it was over, we were all given a pen and paper and wrote 'I walked on fire. I can do anything I choose'. We signed and dated it, a permanent reminder of our 'impossible' achievement.

Affirmations and autosuggestion are very powerful. They give direction to our self-talk, and focus our minds on the things we want. Hundreds of books have been written about them, and you would be forgiven for thinking that they can transform your life by themselves. But experience dictates that this isn't true. Yes, they are enormously helpful, but no, alone they are not sufficient. We confess that we haven't yet told you the whole truth about the firewalk, because in addition to the affirmations, we'd also spent the previous two hours *visualizing* ourselves walking over the coals unharmed. We'll tell you more about 'creative imagery' as we prefer to call it, in the next chapter.

12 Shaping your Future with Creative Imagery

WHATEVER YOUR MIND CAN CONCEIVE AND BELIEVE, YOU CAN ACHIEVE.

Dynamic Living Principle 5

A few years ago, Rex visited Mount Rushmore in the Black Hills of South Dakota, to see the faces of Presidents Washington, Lincoln, Jefferson and Roosevelt carved into its side. He learned that it took the sculptor 14 years to finish the task – truly a labour of love. But this wasn't the only massive sculpture Rex experienced that day. Later in the afternoon, he was taken to see another, of an American Indian riding a horse, shaped out of an entire mountain. It was so high that a ten storey building would easily fit under its armpit. The sculptor had worked on it for no less than 40 years until his death, and his son was now busy completing it. At the bottom of the mountain was a small sign: 'If you can dream it, you can do it.'

This left an indelible impression on Rex. It struck him that everything that has ever been created by the human race originated as a thought or a picture in someone's mind. Any idea, even the briefest flash of insight, that is acted upon for long enough eventually takes a tangible form. The Parthenon, Stonehenge, the Statue of Liberty, the Great Wall of China, the Apollo moon landings, the fax machine – even this book – all started out in exactly the same way; as an idea in someone's mind, which was then brought into reality by physical effort and a great deal of determination and persistence.

Whether we are aware of it or not, we are all continually creating pictures in our minds. Every day, we fantasize about all the things we want, and then forget about them, telling ourselves that it could never happen. If only we could home in on these pictures for long enough, and use them to inspire us and motivate us, they would eventually become our reality.

When Rex set up his first practice, people who used creative imagery were considered eccentric, to say the least. Perhaps they still are in some circles. But Rex was not deterred. Although for several months he had only one patient a week, he would constantly visualize a full appointment book. He would 'see' dozens of people visiting his consulting rooms in his mind's eye. Eventually the practice was treating over 40 patients a day.

Then he started teaching creative imagery to his patients. One of the first was a semi-professional footballer named George, who worked as a junior clerk for a transport company. He had hurt his neck diving into the shallow end of a swimming pool and was in constant pain. George was fascinated to hear how top sports stars were using visualization to improve their performance, and asked Rex to teach him. Soon, he was practising it every night. He would run each match through in his mind in advance, dozens of times, seeing himself scoring prolifically. By the end of the season, despite his team finishing second from bottom, George had become the leading goalscorer in the league and was sought after by several top clubs.

Having tasted success, the ambitious George didn't stop there. If it worked for sport, why not in other areas of his life? As it happened, he was far from happy in his job. He wanted to study for a business degree and set up his own company. 'Would visualization have the same impact on my career?' he wondered. He decided to give it a try. He started visualizing himself running a successful business, and before long, had obtained his degree, left his job and started his own company. Two years later he was a wealthy man, happily married and, remarkably for a man in his late 30s, still a top football player.

In those days, 20 years ago, people would have scoffed if

you had told them that visualization and affirmations were used by:

- Sportsmen and women to help them win races and break world records;
- Business executives to help secure lucrative contracts, make better business presentations and win promotion;
- Patients to rid themselves of serious diseases;
- World famous entertainers to improve their self-confidence and banish stage fright.

But nobody's laughing at these ideas now.

Take, for example, the world of business. Prior to tricky situations such as important sales calls, crucial negotiations, job interviews or presentations to potential clients, many successful executives 'mentally rehearse' while relaxed. They 'see' themselves acting and speaking confidently, signing the contract, accepting the promotion. They hear the audience applauding and bask in the glory of compliments from their colleagues. By the time they come to do it for real, they feel· as if they've done it many times before and the situation holds no fear for them. They are at ease, confident and able to take everything in their stride.

Many years ago, a man named Jim Preston was the president of an American railway company. One day, he paid a visit to a construction site and, by chance, spotted an old colleague, Charlie, laying tracks. Many years earlier, Jim and Charlie had worked together as construction workers, so Jim invited Charlie to have a beer with him. Charlie was very impressed by Jim's rapid rise. 'Hey, Jim', he said, 'I remember the days when we laid tracks together.'

Jim was silent for a moment. He'd never seen it quite like that before. 'You may have been laying tracks, Charlie,' he replied thoughtfully, 'but I was building a railway!'

And here lies the secret of Jim's success, and Charlie's lack of it: Jim had a vision; Charlie had not. Whether he had ever heard the term or not, Jim had used creative imagery.

> *Imagination is the ability to see things as they do not now exist. One possessed with a constructive, positive imagination will see things as he wants them to be. One with negative imagination sees things as he fears they will be.*
>
> Ben Sweetland

Creative imagery is also used widely in top class sport. Cast your mind back to the 1970s and 1980s. Do you recall how East European athletes won nearly everything in sight, and how suspicious Westerners were of their training methods? How did they do it? By brainwashing very young child athletes and artificially stunting their growth? Cheating? Drugs? There were plenty of rumours but few hard facts. The methods used by Eastern bloc athletes had been among the most closely guarded state secrets. It wasn't until the 1990s, when the Berlin Wall came down, that the answer was revealed.

A Bulgarian psychiatrist, Dr Georgi Lozonov, had pioneered a new method of mental training that combined autogenics and mental rehearsal. Lozonov's methods had been adopted throughout the Eastern bloc and were the key to their athletes' success.

Now why this should have been such a surprise in the West is not at all clear, because as early as the 1950s experiments had demonstrated the power of creative imagery in sport. In one very famous example, American students who played basketball once a week were divided into four groups. Each group was tested to see how many baskets they could score from free-throws. They all scored between 21 and 23 percent – about one in five on average.

Then each group was allocated a different training programme for the following month. The first group was told not to practise at all. The second was told to practise free-throws in the gym for three hours a week. The third was instructed not to go near the gym, but to visualize themselves taking free-throws for three hours per week and scoring 100 percent. The fourth was to practise in the gym *and* visualize for three hours per week.

At the end of the month, the students were retested. Not surprisingly, the group that hadn't practised at all showed no improvement. Those who had practised in the gym scored twice as many baskets as before. Astonishingly, so did the group that had only visualized, even though they hadn't touched a basketball for a month.

Clearly, the experiment showed that you can improve as much by practising in your mind as in the gym, but what happens if you do both? Well, the final group, who had both practised *and* visualized, almost trebled their success rate. And just in case you're thinking this was a fluke, we can assure you many similar experiments have been carried out and produced much the same result.

Dr Roger Bannister, the first man to run a mile in under four minutes, mentally rehearsed his historic record attempt hundreds of times before the big day. He once said that he felt a tremendous sense of 'déjà vu' as he rounded the final bend.

Furthermore, when sophisticated biofeedback equipment was used to measure the impact of strenuous activity on athletes' bodies, scientists found that the very same muscles expanded and contracted when they were visualizing as when they were running on the track. So practising in the mind prepares the body for action too.

Visualization has also been used by far-sighted medical practitioners, not only in alternative therapies but also mainstream medicine. Eminent doctors have used it to help patients recover from chronic diseases. Dr Bernie Segal, the famous cancer surgeon and author, has documented hundreds of cases in which patients recovered completely without resorting to conventional treatment such as drugs and chemotherapy.

Two other famous doctor-authors, Carl and Stephanie Simonton, teach their patients to visualize tumours reversing and cancer disappearing. In their book, *Getting Well Again*, they describe how many of their patients were completely cured by their techniques. One was a man with 'incurable' cancer of the throat. Simonton was the last of a long list of doctors to treat him, all the others having given up, but the man quickly rid himself of the cancer using creative mental imagery, then used his new-found skill to cure his arthritis of the knees and impotence. 'I don't need you any more,' he told Simonton. 'I can cure myself.' In similar vein, the eminent heart specialist Dr Dean Ornish, uses creative imagery in conjunction with nutrition, physical exercise and group therapy to clear coronary heart blockages. Needless to say, the conventional medical fraternity, whose answer to most conditions is usually drugs, needles or sharp blades, is lost for an explanation.

Some men see things as they are and say 'Why?' I dream of things that never were and say 'Why not?'

George Bernard Shaw

Creative imagery can be used to treat psychosomatic conditions as varied as blushing, exam nerves, weight problems, bedwetting and lack of confidence, and phobias such as flying, spiders and heights. It can also be used to control pain, reduce the symptoms of stress and promote assertiveness.

All this adds to the mounting evidence that our thoughts and images actually govern our health. If you think of yourself as ill, you'll become ill (if you're not already). Think of yourself as healthy, and your body will respond. This is because wiping out negative thoughts and images and substituting positive ones actually builds the body's autoimmune system, whereas negativity and depression cause it to weaken. Experiments using 'high-tech' measuring devices have proved this. The new science of psycho-neuro-immunology, which has swept the United States, is based on this principle. Isn't it fascinating? Western doctors are calling it '21st-century medicine', although the principle has been accepted and used in the East for thousands of years.

Perhaps you're thinking creative imagery is not really relevant to you if you're in reasonable health or have no wish to be a top sportsperson or business tycoon. If that's your reaction, think again. Remember, you become what you think about, and your thoughts include pictures as well as words. You're thinking, imagining, visualizing all the time whether you like it or not – so why leave things to chance? Why not use this knowledge to shape your life the way you want it, rather than allowing seemingly random thoughts and images to control your destiny?

We know creative imagery works because we use it ourselves. Dave visualized himself as a successful author and speaker years before it became a reality, and Rex has used it every step of the way towards building his practice and becoming a leader in his field. Between us, we have taught it to thousands of people. However, in case you're still a little sceptical, we'd like to explain how and why creative imagery works.

How Creative Imagery Works

As you know, your day-to-day behaviour is determined mainly by your unconscious attitudes. If you want to transform your life, these must be changed, but, unfortunately, once an idea takes root in the unconscious, it's extremely difficult to shift. Your conscious mind is continually sending instructions to the unconscious in the form of words and pictures, and the unconscious does everything in its power to cooperate. If you dwell upon the way things are, you will change nothing. Dwell on your fears, and they will get worse.

Focus on the way you want things to be and the unconscious guides you in a new and exciting direction.

We are all governed by universal 'laws' that have been understood intuitively ever since the dawn of civilization. Unfortunately, most people today are ignorant of them, which doesn't mean they no longer apply, of course. They will influence you just as gravity will pull you to the ground whether you've heard of it or not. There are several dozen such 'laws', but the three most important are the Law of Cause and Effect (which we introduced in Chapter 8), the Law of Attraction and the Law of Projection.

- **The Law of Cause and Effect.** Every thought is a 'cause set in motion' that eventually has a physical effect. Everything starts off as a thought before manifesting in physical form.
- **The Law of Attraction.** Whatever you dwell upon, you will attract into your life. The thoughts and images you hold in your mind will eventually become your reality.
- **The Law of Projection.** The thoughts we send out are picked up by others. We unconsciously attract people into our lives who can help us to achieve our goals and realize our dreams.

Once you have grasped the significance of these universal laws, you will understand the importance of consistently holding clear, positive words and pictures in your mind. Then your unconscious will set to work to help you achieve what you want.

Why words *and pictures*? Simply because for most people (but not everybody), the best way of impressing anything on your unconscious mind is to 'show' it a picture backed up with powerful emotions. Remember, the unconscious is accessed through the right brain, which thinks more clearly in pictures than in words.

There are two further points to bear in mind.

Your Conscious Mind can only Hold One Thought at a Time

It is quite impossible to see two pictures or hold two thoughts in the conscious mind at the same time. If you are clinging to a negative, you are therefore blocking any possibility of focusing on a positive.

The Unconscious cannot Distinguish between Fact and Fantasy

The unconscious is incapable of recognizing whether the conscious mind is feeding it data from the external world via your five senses – sight, hearing, taste, touch and smell – or from your imagination. It will react equally to either. Have you ever cried or been frightened when watching a film? Most people have, even though they were well aware they were watching artificial light flickering on a screen and hearing prerecorded sound. It's exactly the same principle.

If you are not convinced, close your eyes and imagine you are standing at the top of a very tall building, looking over the edge at the tiny figures moving around like ants many storeys below. There is no barrier preventing you from plummeting hundreds of feet and making a nasty mess on the pavement below. Do you have an unpleasant, queasy feeling in your stomach? Can you hear the distant buzz of the traffic, feel the cold wind against your face? What are you thinking? Is your pulse racing?

If you have a good imagination, you will feel little different from how you actually would if you really were peering over the edge of that building. As far as your unconscious mind is concerned, you are there – and it will record the event in your memory as if it really happened.

Now close your eyes again and imagine you are holding a big, juicy lemon. The fresh, tangy, delicate fragrance wafts through the air. Now take a knife and slice the lemon open. Juice runs down your fingers as you raise it to your lips. Is your mouth beginning to water? Does the anticipation of that acidic taste set your teeth on edge? Again, you are reacting as if you were holding a real lemon.

Now let's take the idea a stage further. Once you have impressed your thoughts and images upon your unconscious mind, they are taken up by the Universal Intelligence which co-creates our circumstances with us. It will honour any request, even one made inadvertently. Louise Hay refers to this as 'placing an order in the "cosmic kitchen".' You are guiding cosmic energy to whatever you request. It's like planting a seed. First clear the weeds (the doubts and fears), prepare the ground, add fertilizer, water frequently, and wait. It may take a while for the roots to inch deep into the ground and shoots to appear above the surface, but you must trust that nature is taking its course and be prepared to do whatever is necessary to help it along.

> *We must cultivate our garden. When man was put*
> *in the Garden of Eden, he was put there to work . . .*
> *Let us work without question, that is the only way*
> *to make life tolerable.*
>
> Voltaire

13 Getting the Most from Creative Imagery

Imagination is more important than knowledge.
It is a preview of life's coming attractions.

Albert Einstein

As we have seen, if you want to transform your life, you must recondition your unconscious mind. One way is to use repetition, which is, after all, how your unconscious was programmed in the first place. This means keeping firm control over your self-talk, reciting affirmations regularly, continually focusing on positive thoughts and so on. All these methods work if you persist, but there is a snag. The 'critical censor', situated between the left and right brains, is ever-alert and determined to try and veto any new thoughts which aren't consistent with your existing programming. If you want to speed your progress, you need to find a short cut. You need to bypass the 'critical censor' and feed in new, positive thought-forms. As you've already discovered, the best way is to relax and get into Alpha so that you have a direct line to the right brain. In this tranquil state, your unconscious mind will absorb all the positive words and images you feed into it.

To get the most out of your creative imagery, bear in mind the following ten points.

1 Know What You Want

Before you start, you must clarify your goals. Which area of your life are you working on today? Relationships? Career?

Hobbies? Health? Spiritual growth? You must know what you are trying to achieve before you relax into Alpha, because visualization without a goal is like looking at a map without knowing your destination.

2 Cultivate Desire, Belief and Expectancy

You need to know and understand how to apply these three universal laws.

- **The Law of Desire.** Desire is the strongest positive motivator there is. The more you want something, the more likely you are to succeed. Try writing down as many reasons as possible why you want to achieve your goal, and all the reasons why you *don't* want to fail. This will strengthen your resolve.
- **The Law of Belief.** Whatever you believe, with emotion, becomes your reality, so strong beliefs are essential especially when times are tough. Visualization and affirmations are excellent ways of fostering a strong belief that you can achieve your goal.
- **The Law of Expectancy.** Whatever you expect with confidence becomes a self-fulfilling prophecy. Approach your visualization and affirmations with a firm conviction that you will succeed and you will find your expectations turning to reality.

3 Plan your Sessions

Pick a regular time for your creative imagery sessions and build them into your daily schedule. Then work out the content of each session in advance. If you have difficulty remembering your routine, try recording it and then play it back while you are relaxed.

Remember, also, that you can use the technique any time between sessions, in a kind of guided daydream. Just close your eyes, take a few deep breaths and let the images come flooding into your mind. This is an excellent 'pick-me-up'.

4 Relax

Use your favourite technique from Chapter 6 to go into a relaxed state.

5 Create a Mental Screen

Imagine that you have a screen inside your forehead, just above eye level, rather like a cinema screen. Practise 'watching' images on it until you are totally comfortable and can use it at will. In time, you will find it easy to form a picture, erase it and replace it with another, a useful skill if your mind wanders off. Never picture anything you don't want for more than a few seconds – change it as soon as you can.

6 Allow your Chosen Images to Materialize

The key word here is 'allow'. There is a big difference between the physical work you do, such as digging the garden or cleaning the house, and mental work. Physically, the harder you try, the more you get done, but on the mental plane too much effort can be self-defeating. The gentler the better, so take it easy and allow plenty of time.

7 Make it Big and Bright

Which would you take more notice of, a small, dimly lit black-and-white picture tucked away in the corner of a room, or a large, colourful painting spotlighted in the centre of a wall? Your unconscious will pay more attention if your images are clear, vibrant and animated. Place them at the centre of your mental screen and back them up with autosuggestion.

8 See it through your Own Eyes

It's always best to picture the situation through your own eyes as if you were right there. Let's say you've always wanted to appear on stage at the Sydney Opera House. Imagine yourself in the dress circle watching yourself acknowledging the applause after another inspired performance. Now change your perspective: allow an image of the auditorium in front of you to form *as if you were actually on the stage*. In other words, as a participant, not a spectator. If possible, use all five senses – sight, smell, touch, hearing and taste and really *'be there'*.

It is vital always to imagine yourself reaching perfection, because this is what you want to register in your unconscious memory banks. As with anything, if you can get it right in practice, you're more likely to get it right 'on the night'.

Similarly, if you want a new car, imagine the view as you sit in the driver's seat rather than looking at the car as an observer and seeing yourself at the wheel. If you're a bodybuilder, feel the physical power as you lift another heavy weight above your head.

9 Draw on Powerful Positive Emotions

When you are visualizing, generate as much feeling as you can. Emotions are powerful because they attract energy.

This is another good reason for seeing the scene through your own eyes. It's hard to feel the same intensity of emotion if you're merely observing, because you remain rather detached.

10 *Practise, Practise, Practise*

How do we learn any new skill? There's only one way: to grasp the basics and then practise until they've become second nature. Creative imagery is no different. That's why we recommend that you practise every day. Soon the results will begin to materialize and you'll know you're on your way.

Now take action. If visualizing is as far as you go, nothing will happen and you won't get results. Jim Preston wouldn't have become president of the railway unless he'd worked for it; without hard training, Dr Roger Bannister couldn't have broken the four-minute barrier, and George would not have scored so many goals. Rex wouldn't have attracted sufficient patients if he'd hung around and hoped that somehow they would find their way to him. No, he advertised, went out and gave talks, made contacts with others in a similar field, and, at the same time, perfected his skills. Creative imagery smooths the way to success, but by itself, it isn't enough. In addition, you must do whatever needs to be done.

Four More Techniques

There are literally hundreds of different kinds of creative imagery, but we've selected four of the most useful techniques.

1 *Mirror of the Mind*

The 'Mirror of the Mind' will create new neural pathways in your brain and change your attitudes at a very deep level. You simply create briefly a picture on your mental screen of something you want to move away from, then quickly replace it with an image of what you *do* want. For instance, you can use it to change a bad habit such as overeating, smoking or nailbiting.

Let's take an eating disorder. Create a picture of yourself bingeing on junk food, but make it in dull, drab colours, quite faint and small. Then, in the distance, create an image of a fit and vibrant looking you eating lots of healthy foods, such as fruit, vegetables and salads. Make this picture as bright and colourful as you can, and then gradually draw it towards you while the dull picture fades away into the distance. Soon, the bright picture overwhelms the unwanted image. This is one of the most powerful ways of reconditioning your unconscious mind.

2 *The Swish Technique*

This is similar to the Mirror of the Mind, but with one difference: the negative image is repeatedly replaced by the positive one while you simultaneously make the sound 'swish'. If you think it sounds ridiculous, give it a try; you'll find it really works. It has helped patients suffering from a fear of lifts, flying, needles and heights to conquer this once and for all.

First, create the unwanted image. Imagine you are watching a split-screen production on television or at the cinema. Take the negative picture and shrink it down to the size of a postage stamp on the edge of your mental screen. Now enlarge the positive image until it fills the screen, shattering the negative one, and say 'swish' as if you really mean it. Do it again, at least a dozen times. Your brain will soon get the message to replace the old picture with the new.

3 *Anchoring*

As you know, every experience you've ever had is logged away and can be relived. Why 'relived' rather than *recalled*? Because you are capable of remembering not only the event, but also the emotions you felt at the time.

An anchor triggers a connection between an emotional state

and a specific incident. Is there, for example, a piece of music that evokes happy or sad memories for you? Whenever you hear it, don't all those feelings come flooding back? Is there a particular film which makes you feel nostalgic? Was there a moment in your life when you were so happy that merely thinking about it makes you feel terrific?

Recently, Rex's wife Colleen came across a yellowing slip of paper at the back of a cupboard. Instantly, without knowing why, she was overwhelmed by a heady combination of elation, astonishment and sense of achievement. Then as she examined the faded print, a picture flooded into her mind. She saw herself sitting in front of the radio, listening to a story being read over the air. A story she had written. Suddenly it all came back. When she was 14, she had secretly (knowing her parents would have disapproved) entered a short story competition. She hadn't won, but she had been shortlisted, and received a small prize as well as having her work broadcast on national radio. At the time, she had been almost delirious with excitement. For many years, these feelings had been tucked away in her unconscious, until the sight of her payslip had brought them swarming back to the surface even before her conscious mind had the remotest idea what it was about. The old payslip was a perfect example of a positive anchor.

Anchoring provides a short cut to feeling good whenever you want to: your emotionally-charged memories become a powerful resource to help change your emotional state at will. The anchor itself is usually quite trivial – a gesture, an expression on someone else's face, an old piece of clothing. A mother of grown-up children who browses fondly through old photograph albums of them as babies is using them as an anchor for nostalgic memories.

Anchors are installed and reinforced by repeated use and are most effective if the emotion is strong and the timing right. If you're feeling tired, or indifferent, or agitated, you will not succeed. We'll return to the subject of anchoring in more detail in Chapter 15 (pages 133–4). It's one of the most useful weapons in your armoury of techniques for taking charge of your emotional state. Actors and actresses trained in 'Method Acting' use anchoring (whether they realize it or not) to simulate their characters' emotions. It can work just as well for you, in real life.

4 Reframing

Reframing can be used to lay to rest all the ghosts of the past, all those uncomfortable moments that return to haunt you every now and then. It works because it is never the events themselves that cause you distress, but the way you have perceived them. Change your belief (easier perhaps than you would think), and the problem disappears.

The technique itself is very simple. You run through the event in your mind when in Alpha and give it a different interpretation, one that makes you feel happier. In other words, 'see' it turning out the way you would have wanted. Of course, you'll be aware that the event itself hasn't changed, but, because you feel differently, it will no longer trouble you.

A famous example of reframing occurred in an interview given by Mae West. 'For a long time', she said, 'I was ashamed of the way I lived.' 'Did you reform?' asked the interviewer. 'No,' she replied. 'I'm not ashamed any more.' We're going to return to reframing in Chapter 15 (pages 126–7), because it has a big part to play in dealing with past events which damaged your self-confidence or self-image.

But I Can't Visualize

'That's all well and good,' you might say, 'but I've tried visualizing and I can't do it! I can't see anything at all.' Don't worry, you're not alone, especially if you're new to it. But, in reality, *everyone* can visualize; you're doing it all the time, but often the images come and go so quickly you just don't notice. If you having difficulty, try this approach.

Sit or lie down comfortably. Pick a scene you know well,

perhaps a favourite house or garden. Close your eyes and think of a small part of it – a certain tree, or the front door or a window. Just let an image materialize. If it doesn't, *pretend* you can see it.

Then open your eyes, pause a few seconds, close them and try again. Can you see it? If not, *pretend* you can. Do this a few times. Beginners take heart – you *will* eventually get better at it. Perhaps you're making the mistake of thinking that everyone else can instantly conjure up crystal clear pictures in full technicolour. If so, you're mistaken. Ability to visualize varies enormously; at first, most of us are able to identify nothing more than a hazy image for a few brief moments.

If you've been at it for a while and are still finding it hard, it could be because you're just not a visual person. What do we mean by this? The explanation is rooted in the way different people process (or represent) information. Some of us are visual – that is, we process information using pictures; others are auditory, which means we function better through sound. Others think more in terms of touch, or even smell and taste.

And now we have a confession to make. Neither of us is able to visualize in the sense of being able to *see* clear pictures, but the technique still works for us. We *imagine*, feel, even hear the sounds we associate with our goals. For example, the first launderette Rex owned used second-hand equipment that was long past its best. Every day, he would imagine owning a beautiful new launderette in smart premises with brand new equipment, frequented by myriads of customers. He was never able to picture what it *looked* like, but he had a sense of what it would *be* like. He got better and better at imagining it and, of course, it eventually materialized.

So, rest assured that creative imagery will work equally well if you're not visual. However, in reality, nobody is 100 percent dominated by any one sense. We usually combine our preferred representational system with a little of the others. So if you have difficult visualizing, don't worry, use sound (such as words or affirmations) or touch instead and it will be just as effective. Whatever you're most comfortable with is absolutely right for you because it's the way your brain works.

Are Creative Imagery and Affirmations Infallible?

Sometimes we set aside the time for visualization and faithfully recite our affirmations – and nothing seems to happen! Or occasionally, disappointed clients say, 'It hasn't got the results I wanted. Why won't it work for me?' There are a number of reasons, which crop up time and time again.

- Desire, belief and expectancy aren't strong enough.
- Persistence is lacking or insufficient time allowed.
- Visualizations or affirmations are poorly framed.
- You are trying too hard; remember, with mental work, the less effort, the better.
- Doubts creep in – 'It may not work. Perhaps I won't get what I want?' Doubt and disbelief take you right back where you started and mean you have to place your order with the 'Cosmic Kitchen' all over again.

However, there is another reason why we don't always get what we want immediately: perhaps something better awaits us. Wise people know that 'God's delays are not God's denials'. The Universal Intelligence is smarter than us: it knows better than we do what is in our long-term interests. Perhaps this is what George Bernard Shaw meant when he said, 'There are two tragedies in life. One is not to get your heart's desire. The other is to get it.'

Recently our colleague, Joanne, was trying to buy an apartment. She visualized and affirmed several times a day, but wasn't able to borrow enough money to clinch the deal. Then, just as she was beginning to despair, the vendor rang up and reduced the price by £3,000 for a quick sale. Now she could afford it.

So be flexible and keep an open mind. You're harnessing powerful energies, so don't misuse them. Follow the example of our friend Marie who always adds, 'This, or something better, I accept for myself, for my greatest good and the greatest good of all.' Don't forget, you are unblocking the mental barriers you have erected through conditioning and ineffectual thinking, so that you get back in tune with the flow of life itself. Only then will life start to work the way you want it to.

Now I see that creative visualization and
affirmations don't make anything happen at all.
What they do is help to dissolve our barriers,
fears and negative beliefs that keep us from allowing the
goodness of life to happen to us.

Shakti Gawain

The Dynamic Living Formula

You now know the first four elements of the Dynamic Living Formula, the basic toolkit you need for transforming your thinking:

1 Physical relaxation
2 Mental calm
3 Positive self-talk
4 Creative imagery

Memorize them, practise them, use them. The fifth element, the 'as if' principle will be explained in Chapter 17 (page 148).

You will then be able to use this formula to help you become, have or do anything you want. But first there is one thing you need. Without it, your chances of being healthy, happy or successful are slim. It is your springboard to everything you want to achieve in life. In fact, it is so important that the next three chapters are devoted to it.

14   The Most Important Judgement You'll Ever Make

*Self-esteem isn't everything, it's just
that there's nothing without it.*

Gloria Steinem

Of all the judgements we make, none is more important than
the value we place on ourselves. Health, happiness and success are beyond our grasp without self-love, confidence and
self-esteem. They are absolutely fundamental to everything.

Let's take some examples. Think back to Chapter 2 and the
five life areas: physical/health, finance/career, social/ relationships, leisure/recreation and spiritual/self-development.

- **Health.** Doctors agree that stress is behind more than 80
  percent of illness; and low self-esteem is behind more than
  80 percent of stress. It is at the root of every psychological
  problem. This was driven home to us recently when an
  experienced nurse at a local psychiatric hospital told us
  that she couldn't recall a single patient whose self-esteem
  was high.
- **Finance and career.** People with low self-esteem *always*
  underachieve at work. It's a myth that earnings and promo-
  tions depend on your *qualifications*. They are much more
  closely tied to your *self-confidence*.

  There's a very simple reason for this: your self-image is a
  bit like the thermostat that controls your central heating.
  When the house gets too cold, it switches the heating on,
  and when it gets too warm, it goes off again. Similarly, if we
  feel we're not living up to our expectations, we try harder;
  but if we believe we're doing better than we have any right
  to because our self-esteem is low, we slacken off. Since we

can never really rise above the level of our own self-image, this effectively places a glass ceiling on our achievements.

- **Social and relationships.** People with low self-esteem *always* have relationship problems. It's the fundamental cause of marriage breakdown, parent–child friction and most sexual problems. If you don't love yourself, how can you possibly have genuine love for another? Improve your self-esteem and your relationships will surely follow.

- **Leisure and recreation.** High self-esteem is your spring-board to a full and adventurous life. People who feel good about themselves are prepared to take risks, try new things and meet new people. They are also likely to be much more successful at sport.

- **Spiritual and self-development.** People with low self-esteem rarely spend time working on themselves – deep down, they just don't think they're worth the effort. Those with high self-esteem enjoy improving themselves physically, mentally, emotionally and spiritually, and are prepared to work at it.

Without self-esteem, life will always be a bit of a burden to you and you'll always feel like a victim. Remember Dynamic Living Principle number 6? Without any doubt, a feeling of self-worth and confidence are the first qualities to work on. But take heart: self-confidence is a *decision* that you make for yourself. Anyone – yes, anyone, including you – can have confidence. How do we know? We've done it ourselves. Rex remembers what it was like to be bullied and to resort to drinking in an attempt to capture the self-confidence he lacked when he was sober. He's not bullied now, and he hasn't touched alcohol in over 20 years. And Dave looks back almost in disbelief to the days when he felt so worthless that he was afraid to go to a party or speak up for himself!

The Roots of Low Self-Esteem

Our self-concept begins to take shape before we are out of the cradle. In fact, psychologists generally agree that it is pretty well established by the time we reach the tender age of eight. This puts a daunting responsibility on parents, compounding an already difficult job. The average child of 12 has already received around 25 thousand hours of parental input, and an alarmingly high proportion (90 percent) is negative. This 90 percent is often made up of the usual run-of-the-mill admonitions and reprimands – 'Don't do that', 'Be careful or else', 'No you can't' – but the accumulated effect over many years can be devastating. No wonder children gradually lose their enthusiasm, curiosity, courage, and – most important – their belief in themselves.

> *The first half of our lives is ruined by our parents, and the second half by our children.*

Clarence Darrow

Mary was a typical case. Under hypnosis, it emerged that as a small child she had been so traumatized by a barrage of parental verbal battering (no doubt well-intentioned) that by the age of six she was quite unable to speak up for herself. She recalled how another six-year-old had deliberately run his toy car over her head and she had literally been unable to open her mouth and say 'Don't do that'.

A later incident at the age of nine, when she was yelled at in public for getting lost at the cinema, continued to haunt her for many years. (Her parents, of course, had probably forgotten all about it by the same evening.) Trivial events such as these can do untold damage to a sensitive child. By her own admission, Mary was unable to say 'boo' to a goose and, even after she grew up, she could not dismiss her parents' censure. For instance, when they felt she was unsuitable for the career she had in mind, she dropped all her plans, feeling unable to pursue it.

Children like Mary are made to feel that they are loved only when doing what their parents approve of, rather than for themselves. They quickly learn to interpret 'Do as I tell you, or else' as 'unless you do what I expect, you won't be wanted or loved.' Such children may still be unconsciously trying to win Mum and Dad's approval long after they have grown up and left home. Alternatively, frustrated at not being able to get through to their parents, they may switch their attention to other people and try to win their approval instead.

Mary's parents were ordinary well-meaning people, blissfully unaware that they were doing anything but the best for their daughter. Children like Mary have only one hope – consciously and deliberately to work on their self-esteem until they have overcome their poor start in life. Fortunately, with Rex's help, Mary was able to work through and throw off all the emotional junk she was carrying.

Many adolescents are put off their ambitions by shortsighted adults with 'play it safe' attitudes. Ask a small child what she wants to be when she grows up. Perhaps she's just been watching a Grand Prix on television. Fired with imagination, she replies, 'A racing driver like Nigel Mansell.' At that moment, the chances of failure or danger don't even enter her head – she's consumed with enthusiasm and excitement. How does a typical adult, caught up in the moment, respond? 'That's terrific, I'll be so proud of you when you're the World Champion!'

But ten years later, the reaction is quite different. The child is now 15 years old and it's time to choose her options at school. 'I've always wanted to be a racing driver,' she says. 'How do I get to become one?'

'Don't be so silly, you haven't a hope and, besides, it's no career for a girl. What you need are some qualifications, then find a steady job with good prospects, security and a pension plan. There's so much unemployment around, you've got to think of the future. And you'll probably want to settle down, get married and have children one day.' She sighs. That's not what she wants at all, but she's rapidly becoming resigned to it.

People are naturally suspicious of anything that lies outside their own experience, and it shows in the guidance they give to their children. Many sporting heroes, successful entertainers, writers, artists and inventors would have taken 'safe' jobs if they'd listened to their parents.

Returning to childhood, Dennis Waitely, a top motivational consultant, still recalls his pre-school days when his grandfather would tuck him up in bed every night. 'He would say things like, 'Dennis, you are the most wonderful boy in the world. One day you're going to be a great man. I love you very much and when you fall asleep tonight, all the lights all over the world will go out at the very same moment.' With all those positive words echoing in my mind building me up day after day, it's no surprise that I grew up wanting to do the same for others!'

This is a charming little story, but even if you feel you were damaged by negative input, and your self-esteem has hit rock-bottom, take heart: it doesn't have to stay that way. You always have a choice. Take John and Lorraine, who are brother and sister. Their father was a wealthy local businessman with a dubious reputation. He had twice been to jail, once for attacking a rival with a baseball bat and a second time for dealing in stolen goods. They'd never seen much of him because he was always out 'on business', although their mother often wondered what kind of business he was engaged in. She eventually discovered that he'd had a string of affairs.

When his father was sent to prison for the second time, John, who was 16 at the time, decided he wasn't going to end up like that. He didn't want to be tarred with the same brush, so he worked hard at school, went to college and joined a local engineering company. By the time he was in his late 20s, he'd made it to middle management and bought a house. His spare time was devoted to tennis, sailing and playing music, and he had a hectic social life. Ask him how he was and he would always reply, 'Couldn't be better'.

But Lorraine was very different. As a teenager, she felt the world was against her. The older she got, the more resentful she became. Although no less talented than her brother, she dropped out of school early and drifted in and out of a series of menial jobs (none of which she enjoyed). She also went from one down-and-out boyfriend to another, all of whom left her because of her unpredictable moods and bad temper. She felt worthless, and envied her brother his success. 'He's just lucky,' she once said. 'Males always are.'

John and Lorraine were once asked, independently, why they thought their lives had taken the course they had, and both gave the same reply: 'What would you expect with a father like mine?'

> *Children begin by loving their parents.*
> *After a time, they judge them.*
> *Rarely, if ever, do they forgive them.*
>
> Oscar Wilde

Self-esteem is simply a Belief about Yourself

The example of John and Lorraine shows that it's not the events and circumstances in your past that determine your level of self-esteem, but your *beliefs* about them. Where do these beliefs come from? Primarily your conditioning, but also your interpretation of your experiences, the knowledge you have gained along the way and results you've achieved. All these factors help shape your opinion of your ability:

Results come from your
  Behaviour which is a result of your
    Feelings which are influenced by your
      Attitudes which spring from your
        Beliefs which arise mainly from your
          Conditioning.

Have you ever given up on something that you enjoyed or cared about, or abandoned a cherished personal goal, because you were discouraged – either by someone else or by your own feelings of inadequacy? Do you ever remember thinking, 'I'm just no good at this', and then dropping out? The real reason why you quit was not that you weren't any good, but that you *believed* you weren't any good. Your beliefs govern your reality and send a direct order to the unconscious to 'make it so'. This principle is summarized in one of the universal mental laws which you have already met:

- **The Law of Belief.** Whatever you believe, with emotion, becomes your reality.

There is, however, another way that beliefs can be formed. *You can consciously and deliberately create them.* You can also change a belief that isn't working for you.

All your beliefs are learned, and what is learned can be *un*learned. When you were born, your mind was a clean slate. Your beliefs and conditioning were acquired and modified as you grew up. Do you remember when you believed a fat old man with a long white beard wearing a red coat came down your chimney every Christmas Eve and left presents? You don't believe that any longer, do you? Do you still believe in the tooth fairy? Beliefs are changing all the time, sometimes dramatically. How about people who experience sudden religious conversions in adulthood?

> *Men often become what they believe themselves to be. If I believe I cannot do something, it makes me incapable of doing it. When I believe I can, I acquire the ability to do it even if I didn't have it in the beginning.*

> Mahatma Gandhi

You can change your beliefs using the Dynamic Living techniques you've already encountered, plus a few more you'll come across in the next two chapters. We'll return to them later.

The Different Faces of Your Self-image

The image you have of yourself may not be accurate. Nor may it be anything like how you appear to other people. Of course, your self-image varies according to the situation. For instance, as a boy Dave had no problems passing exams or playing the piano in front of large audiences, but would freeze with fear at the thought of approaching a stranger. He had a good intellectual self-image but a poor social self-image. You also have a physical, an emotional, a real and an ideal self-image. Let's take a look at each of these in turn.

Physical Self-image

Most of us could easily produce a list of what we see as our physical shortcomings, but grow extremely reticent when asked to say what we think is right about our appearance. Perhaps we simply don't want anyone to think we're conceited. Whether you like it or not, others do respond to physical appearance, so you might as well accept it. Just remember to play up your good points and play down your bad ones. Everybody has bad points. Even the most renowned beauties don't always look so good first thing in the morning.

There are, of course, a myriad of ways to change your appearance if you really want to, some of them quite drastic, but before you rush out to the plastic surgeon, remember what Coco Chanel once said to a client: 'Be careful of looking in the mirror, my dear. It only reflects what you think of yourself.'

Emotional Self-image

Are you generally a happy, enthusiastic, positive person? Or are you a habitual worrier, prone to angry outbursts or (even worse) riddled with guilt?

Negative emotions, as you know, are very destructive, and

they will destroy your self-esteem as surely as a fire engulfing a dry forest. To feel good about yourself, find reasons for fanning the fires of enthusiasm for living that are smouldering deep within you.

Intellectual Self-image

In an experiment once carried out in the 1950s, a group of students who were good at mathematics but poor at English quietly and unbeknown to them had their exam results switched round. They were told that they had a definite flair for English, but weren't quite up to the mark in mathematics. What do you think happened? That's right, they went through school living up to their own and their teachers' expectations. Then the researchers did a similar switch on another group who were good at English but weak at maths. Some bright students who had been led to believe they were no good at English actually failed it.

It's frightening to think that you might have been told by a thoughtless teacher or parent in junior school that 'you'll never amount to anything', and here you are, 20 or 30 years later, still believing that you just don't have what it takes! It can happen so easily.

But, of course, it works both ways. The one redeeming feature of the 1950s' experiment was that the kids who originally weren't good at mathematics or English did well in both subjects. Because their teachers treated them as though they were gifted pupils, they responded accordingly. Their 'actual', pre-experiment level of competence doesn't matter now, does it? Think about this, and don't restrict yourself with false, self-destructive beliefs!

Social Self-image

Do you worry about what other people think of you? Do you ever feel used, patronized, disliked, looked down upon? Do you enjoy social situations, or would you rather keep yourself to yourself, believing that you're no good in company? Relax. Most people are far too busy worrying about what *you* think of *them* to spend time judging you.

The (perhaps uncomfortable) fact is that *people always treat you exactly the way you teach them to*. If you feel downtrodden, it's because you've behaved like a doormat. If you feel taken advantage of, it's because you've (however unintentionally) given out the message that you're available to be used.

Basically, you get back what you give out. If you want others to respect you, have respect for yourself. Start behaving differently and you'll probably find they start treating you better. What you think of *yourself* is what really matters.

> *What you think of me is*
> *none of my business.*
>
> Terry Cole-Whittaker

Real versus Ideal Self-image

How big is the gap between the person you think you are (your 'real' self-image) and the person you would like to be (your 'ideal' self-image)?

Your 'real' self-image dictates your behaviour and governs your degree of success in every area of your life. But there is nothing to stop you breaking away from your 'real' self-image and working towards your 'ideal' self-image. High self-esteem is not a gift bestowed upon some favoured people by a strangely partisan deity, it is a decision you make. Self-confidence is not something you inherit in your genes, it is something you *choose to have*. Most people need some assistance in making that decision (see the next chapter). But first, one of the most important steps.

Forgiving Your Parents

Blaming your parents, teachers and so on won't help. After all, they were products of their conditioning too and what may have seemed like a personal vendetta against you was really just ignorance on their part. But you're different, aren't you? You're going to step in and break this chain of mental abuse that's been handed down unwittingly from generation to generation. Not necessarily because *they* deserve it – perhaps they don't. We know some parents do dreadful things to their children, but that isn't the point. It's because *you* deserve it. Failing to forgive gives them the power to affect your life now, and you owe it to yourself to be free of all the resentment and bitterness you've been carrying around with you. It's not helping you, so release it. You're your own parent now. Yes, from now on, *you* are 100 percent responsible for yourself.

If you haven't forgiven your parents,
you haven't left home.

Anon

15 Creating Confidence

In quietness and confidence
shall be your strength.

Isaiah 30:15

An investment in building your self-esteem is nothing less than an investment in life itself. You *owe* it to yourself to have high self-esteem, and you are the only one who can do it. Whatever you think of yourself right now, you can raise your self-esteem.

Take Chris, for example, a young man torn by inner conflict, a longing to succeed doing battle with a self-destructive urge which was driving him to the edge of a complete breakdown. He would sit up night after night until the early hours, aimlessly plucking the bristles from a broom. Everything seemed a disaster. His relationship with his girlfriend was virtually over, he loathed his job, his life was going nowhere. At the root of his problem was an intense self-hatred. He saw himself as a failure, and had hit the depths of depression.

Chris was one of Rex's greatest challenges (and ultimately one of his greatest successes). He delved into his past and helped him understand and come to terms with the reasons for his current problems. He taught him the Dynamic Living Principles and techniques, and encouraged him to help himself. It gave Rex great pleasure to see him gradually gaining insight and using his new-found skills to make changes. After a few months, Chris left his job and started a small business. He worked tirelessly and built it up into a nationwide concern, eventually selling it for a large sum when he was offered an executive position with a major company.

For a long time Chris had felt he was a prisoner of his past conditioning. But of course he was simply trapped by negative thinking patterns. All he needed was the self-awareness and discipline to make the effort to gain control of his thoughts. Then his life started to change and he began to feel like a master rather than a victim of his circumstances.

If Chris could do it, anybody can. We are going to give you the same techniques and principles for personal change that he used.

*You have no idea what a poor opinion I have
of myself – and how little I deserve it!*

W S Gilbert

Negative and Positive Spirals

Our behaviour evokes a response in others that reinforces our self-image. It works like this. If, for instance, we behave confidently, others assume we have confidence and treat us accordingly. This makes us feel even more confident and it reflects in our behaviour.

On the other hand, if we behave *un*confidently, others assume we are unconfident and treat us as such, which robs us of what little confidence we do have. It's a self-perpetuating spiral which must be broken, and the best way is to behave confidently, even if it feels like an act to begin with. You will soon enjoy the feeling of competence and self-respect that follows. Simultaneously, you should use mental reconditioning (positive self-talk, creative imagery and so on) to change your perception of yourself.

If this sounds like a tall order, don't worry. There's an easily remembered, five-step process you can use. We call it the 'Five As: Awareness, Acceptance, Attitude, Appreciation, Action. Creating confidence using the Five As is what this chapter is all about.

1 Awareness

First you need to understand *why*, *where* and *when* you lack self-esteem. Are certain situations more daunting than others? If so, who said what to you when you were young and impressionable, and why? You need to sort this one out in your mind and put everything in perspective. Don't forget, the reason behind all the negative input was not any shortcoming within yourself.

Try asking yourself some searching questions. Take a sheet of paper and work through each of the following. Write six to ten answers to each question very rapidly, avoiding straight 'yes' or 'no' answers where possible, and without pondering over them too much. It also helps if you look in a mirror as you're doing it. When you've finished, read through the answers and digest their meaning:

1 One of the things I *like* most about myself is . . .
2 One of the things I *dis*like most about myself is . . .
3 I like myself *most* when . . .
4 I like myself *least* when . . .
5 Does the work I do satisfy my need for fulfilment and creativity? If not, what steps can I take to correct the situation?
6 Am I content with my circle of friends and my intimate relationships? In what way(s) could they be improved?
7 Am I happy with my health and my physical appearance? In what way(s) can they be improved?
8 Do I take responsibility for my own decisions or do I allow other people to push me around?
9 Do I have a sense of purpose about my life that benefits others as well as myself? Am I doing all that I can to fulfil it?
10 Is my self-talk positive or negative? How can I improve it?
11 Have I struck a good balance between work and leisure? if not, what can I do to correct it?
12 In which situations do I feel comfortable and competent? In which do I feel uneasy and unable to cope?

13 How do I feel about my intellectual make-up?
14 How do I feel about my emotions?
15 How do I feel about my way of dealing with other people, including social situations?

Another useful exercise is to make a list of your good and bad points. Take a sheet of paper and draw a line down the middle. Write all the qualities you like about yourself on one side, and all the things you dislike on the other. If you find it easier to list your weaknesses and mistakes rather than your strengths and proud accomplishments, you've got work to do!

Have a look at the positive traits. If you met someone who had those qualities, what would you think of them? Would you be impressed? Then why are you so critical of yourself?

Now – what robbed you of your self-esteem? Remember, your purpose is to *identify* the reasons, not to attach blame. It helps if you go into Alpha at this point, because your ability to see things in their true perspective will be heightened. Reflect on whether you could have handled awkward situations differently. What did you learn from them? Would you handle them differently if a similar situation arose now?

This last question provides you with a good opportunity to make the most of the 'reframing' technique. As you'll recall from Chapter 13, reframing is a way of changing how you feel about past unhappy events. It's not difficult to do, once you've got the idea.

1 Go into Alpha.
2 Run the scene through in your mind, but change the ending. See it *as you would have liked it to be*. Don't forget to conjure up all the appropriate emotions. With repeated practice, your mind will accept this as reality and, should a similar event ever arise, you will react more positively.
3 Alternatively, change your belief about it. For example, Jeremy thought he had a problem talking to people. Whenever he was in company, he felt left out of the conversation.

He concluded that he was boring and nobody liked him. With a little probing, it turned out that most of his acquaintances were interested in sport – which he wasn't – and this was usually the main topic of conversation. He then saw his so-called problem more clearly: he wasn't a social misfit, he was mixing with people who didn't share his interests, especially in the arts. He used affirmations and creative imagery to 'see' himself with a new circle of art-loving friends. Like all these techniques, it didn't work instantly, but within a few months his social life was transformed.

Changing your beliefs about an event can be facilitated by asking yourself four simple questions:

1 What else could this (situation, memory, behaviour, etc.) mean?
2 How else could it be described?
3 What positive value could it have?
4 What have I learned from it that will benefit me in future?

You can't change the past, but you can change your perception of it so that it need not disempower you any more. This is the purpose of reframing. Your *conscious* mind understands the reality perfectly well, and knows that you are simply changing your thinking, but your *unconscious* cannot distinguish between fact and fantasy. It is quite happy to accept the new scenario and feed back all the confident, happy emotions you need.

2 Acceptance

Of course, there are some things about yourself that you can never change. If you are 5 foot 2 inches and would rather be 6 foot 2 inches, you are just going to have to learn to live with it. Why waste your time and energy fretting over something that you can do nothing about?

> *God, give us grace to accept with serenity the*
> *things that cannot be changed, courage to change*
> *the things which should be changed, and the*
> *wisdom to distinguish the one from the other.*

Reinhold Niebuhr

Some things are much easier to change than others, although people go to great lengths to hide the truth (for example facelifts to hide the effects of ageing). The secret, though, is to focus on what you can change and on what you already do well. For instance, one of Dave's younger clients was very contemptuous of herself except for one thing – her physical appearance. He encouraged her to make the most of her assets and one day she spotted an entry form for a modelling competition. First prize was a year at modelling school followed by six months' guaranteed work. She persuaded a friend to take some photographs of her and entered. To her surprise (but not Dave's) she won, and enjoyed every moment of her training. Her self-esteem in all areas has already risen several hundred percent.

3 Attitude

Most of your achievements are due to your attitude, not your physical attributes, intelligence and so on. With the right attitude, you can make a success of almost anything you attempt. Of course, attitude is closely tied to your beliefs, and self-esteem boils down to a set of beliefs about yourself, based on your thinking patterns. Cast your mind back to the Law of Cause and Effect. Right cause – right effect. Right thinking – right action. Right attitude – right result. On the other hand, if you *think* you're unworthy or incapable of something, you're in the grip of a self-fulfilling prophecy.

It's vital to examine your beliefs about yourself and change any that are negative. For instance, we often hear our clients say:

> '*I'm too old/young.*'
> '*I'm not talented/clever/good enough.*'
> '*I'm not attractive/strong/tall/sexy enough.*'
> '*I'm too shy/sensitive/introverted.*'
> '*People like me aren't born to win/be loved/be happy.*'
> '*I know I'm weak/stupid/ugly but it's just the way I am.*'

What do you think these beliefs do to a person? Have you any similar beliefs? If so, you'd better start working on them immediately. You can draw on the full battery of Dynamic Living techniques.

Use *relaxation into Alpha* to contact your inner wisdom and allow your unconscious mind to be receptive to new, positive thoughts and images about yourself.

Use *mindfulness* to observe your thoughts when relaxed and continuously monitor your thinking and feelings during the day.

Use *conscious thought stopping* to get rid of negative and self-pitying thoughts and make room for positive ones.

Use *positive self-talk* to recondition old beliefs by taking charge of your inner dialogue. Be sure never to say anything about yourself, either silently or out loud, that you don't sincerely want to be true. Make this an incontrovertible rule from now on. Use all the self-talk techniques.

- **Wordpower** – be sure to choose your words very carefully to reinforce your good feelings about yourself and change destructive thoughts into empowering ones.
- **Positive questions** – give your Prover the right ammunition by ensuring your internal interrogation always leads to a positive answer.
- **Affirmations** – frame affirmations that feel right for you and repeat them frequently, using mirror-work, sticky labels, cassette tapes or any other aids that you find helpful.

Remember the Five Ps. Here are some suggestions to get you started.

'I like myself.'
'I am a strong and worthy person.'
'I have all the qualities I need.'
'I am loving, lovable and loved.'
'I automatically and joyfully focus on the positive.'
'I feel warm and loving towards myself.'
'I am worthy of all the good in my life.'
'I think, talk and act with confidence at all times.'
'I believe in myself. I can do anything I choose.'
*'If I apply myself with determination, persistence and
   enthusiasm, I know I will succeed.'*
'I like who I am. I'm glad to be me.'

- **Autosuggestion** – to enhance their effectiveness, recite your affirmations when in Alpha, or listen to a prerecorded cassette tape.

Use *creative imagery* to 'see', 'hear' and 'sense' yourself as a confident and successful person. Conjure up pictures of yourself in the Mirror of the Mind and use the Swish technique (page 106) to replace outdated images. Try this three-stage approach:

- 'Visualize' yourself as a confident person and imagine what it would feel like to be loaded with confidence.
- Next, visualize yourself behaving with assurance, walking tall, moving and relating to others confidently.
- Finally, visualize yourself having accomplished your ambition entirely to your satisfaction.

Get into the habit of mentally rehearsing any challenge you face, 'seeing' yourself winning through every time. Practise these routines often enough and it won't be long before they become reality.

4 Approval

Self-approval is the conviction that you are a valuable person, capable and lovable (even if others haven't yet noticed it!). Apart from positive self-talk and other techniques, here's one more way to cultivate solid self-worth:

- Make a list of all your good points and read it through frequently.
- Record it and play the tape when you're relaxing.
- List all your faults, then cross each one out and replace it with its opposite.
- Memorize both lists. They will give your unconscious something to work on.

You'll find that most of your so-called faults are simply learned responses or bad habits acquired over the years, which will fall away as you begin to correct your thinking. So constantly remind yourself of your good points and the progress you're making, list your achievements and always focus on your potential rather than your limitations.

5 Action

Building something from your own idea is the best possible way to live. The inner applause you give yourself when you succeed outweighs anything anyone could ever give you.

Leonard Abrahamson

Now you're ready for action. Without taking practical steps, your new-found confidence will be like an aeroplane glued to the runway – full of potential but unable to fly. The secret is to act 'as if' you are the kind of person you want to be.

Let's imagine for a moment that all your strengths and talents were fully developed and all your weaknesses eliminated.

What would you *feel* like? What would you *be* like? Keep an impression of this 'perfect' you in your mind and behave as if you're already there. The more you act as if you are confident, the more confident you will become and the more others will perceive you as a confident person.

Constantly think winning thoughts. Back them up with positive physiology – a confident posture, walking tall, shoulders squared, a confident expression on your face and assured tone of voice. Actors know that the body can help to conjure up any emotion. Try it! How would you stand if you were feeling unbeatable? What would your facial expression be? William Shakespeare summed it up: 'Assume a virtue if you have it not.' It will become part of you.

Further Techniques

There are two more techniques you can use to help you. The first is 'modelling' and the second you have already come across – 'anchoring'.

Modelling

If you want to change your behaviour and/or acquire new skills, it helps if you have a 'model' in your mind's eye, someone whom you admire and would like to emulate. This could be a real person, or a vision of yourself as the very best that you can be. Find out as much as you can about that other person and observe them in action. Imagine what it must be like to *be* them. If it's somebody you know, or someone famous you're lucky enough to meet, ask them how they built their confidence. You'll gain some valuable hints; you'll probably also discover that they're not always as confident as they seem. Even highly successful people draw on the 'as if' principle at times.

A word of warning. Don't expect to copy your role model exactly. You will never do it quite like them because you'll put your own individual stamp on it. Your own combination of experiences, character traits, skills, talents and so on will give you your own individual style, not necessarily better or worse than the next person's, just different. And talent is always only half the story. The essential ingredients of success are determination, self-discipline, drive and staying power – the ability to see the job through.

Anchoring

Anchors can be used whenever you want to feel confident. By drawing on memories of past successes, (and everybody has some), you can re-create those feelings very quickly. Your emotionally-charged memories are a powerful resource for changing your emotional state at will.

First, you install the anchor by 're-experiencing' the event when in Alpha. When the feelings are really intense, choose and install your anchor. It could be a tug on the ear lobe, touching your Adam's apple, pinching yourself on the arm or whatever, accompanied by a unique word or phrase such as '1, 2, 3, confident!' or 'yes, yes, I *can*!'

Then, when you want to feel and behave confidently, activate your anchor by repeating the trigger action or phrase precisely as you used it when the anchor was installed. It's very important to repeat it exactly, otherwise the anchor may not 'hook'. If you are successful, you will find all those empowering feelings surfacing again, just as they did before. Anchors are originated and reinforced by repetition and are most effective when you can simulate strong emotion. An attempt at anchoring when you are feeling indifferent will not succeed, and an anchor which has not been used for some time will lose its power and fade away. You must 'use it or lose it!'

Let's give an example. Suppose you have been asked to give a speech to a large audience including some important local dignitaries. You once gave a successful talk at an informal gathering, which was so well received that you felt a tremendous sense of pleasure and pride which lasted for weeks.

Relax. Take your mind back to the successful talk. When you're focusing on the feelings you want to re-create, put your thumb and fingers together, and say 'Yes! Confident!' (or any phrase that suits you) in a strong tone of voice. Then 'see', 'hear' and 'sense' yourself giving your forthcoming talk, looking, sounding and acting totally assured. Do this several times, two or three times a day, especially the night before.

Just before you are called upon to speak, activate your anchor. This may sound like a conjuring trick, but all you're actually doing is giving a little help to a perfectly natural process which has been going on all your life. We highly recommend it and have used it frequently ourselves. For instance, Dave was once asked to deliver a lecture programme through an interpreter to a large audience at a business school in Moscow on a subject he knew little about. Although he had no idea what to expect, he used techniques such as relaxation, anchoring and mental rehearsal. The lectures were a great success and many people admired his confident delivery.

Self-confidence is not something you have, but a feeling you can create and develop. It starts when you take a few small steps at a time and 'have a go'. Being properly prepared increases the chances of success. Build on your strengths, and devote yourself to something you do well. Each small victory will give you encouragement, and before long you'll feel better than ever before.

Self-confidence, like happiness, is slippery when we set out to grab it for its own sake. Usually it comes as a by-product. We lose ourselves in service or work, friendship or love, and suddenly we realize we are confident and happy.

Alan Loy McGinnis

16 Living Confidently

No one can make you feel inferior
without your consent.

Eleanor Roosevelt

Success, as you know, is largely determined by your self-image. If you have high self-esteem, you will feel that you deserve the best. You will cope better with life's hard knocks, and see them as the challenges and opportunities for learning they really are. But, unless you want to be a lighthouse keeper or professional hermit, you're going to have to deal with other people. You will have to cope with their expectations of you, handle criticism and sometimes manage rejection without letting it affect you. Your relationships with others are the arena in which your self-esteem is tested, the surest measure of your own feelings of self-worth and confidence.

The most important relationship you will ever have is the one with yourself. If you feel safe and secure with who you are, you will not be vulnerable to unfair criticism from others, and you will not be overly critical of yourself. You will take responsibility for your own thoughts and actions, and judge yourself by your own criteria, not other people's. Above all, you will be your own person and have no need to pander to anyone.

The first thing to realize is that you do not have to get on well with everyone. To think that you do is unrealistic and will lead to disappointment. It is inevitable that you will meet people you like and who like you, and it is very gratifying when this happens. But you will also meet others with whom you have little in common; you might as well accept that you will never see eye to eye with them. You cannot please all of the people all of the time.

When Margaret Thatcher became UK Prime Minister for the third time in 1987 with a majority of over 150 seats in the House of Commons, it was hailed as one of the greatest political victories of all time. Can you recall the proportion of the vote she attracted that year? 42 percent! Think about it – we call 42 percent a 'landslide', yet how many people feel bad about themselves if they don't get on with 100 percent of the people they encounter. Even your best friends won't approve of you all the time!

You can easily gauge a person's level of self-esteem by the way they relate to others. Here are some tell-tale signs of low self-esteem.

Craving recognition and approval from others is a sure sign. It can take many forms, but usually involves constantly doing (or saying) things simply to please others. If you're not sure whether you are in this position, ask yourself: 'If there were nobody else in the world, would I still follow this path?' If your answer is 'yes' – wonderful! Go ahead: your reasons are valid.

There's no point in being a conformist for conformity's sake (or even a rebel for the sake of it) or pretending to be what you're not. Other people will like and respect you more for your individuality than your passive acquiescence. If, for instance, you find yourself in the company of a group of classical music enthusiasts, don't pretend to like opera if you've never got beyond rock'n'roll. The group will appreciate your honesty, and don't be surprised if one of them takes you aside later and whispers, 'Don't tell anyone, but I've always secretly preferred the Beatles to Beethoven!'

Of course, there is nothing wrong with basking in the glow of a sincerely-paid compliment or a few words of praise from somebody you respect. But it becomes a serious problem if the need for approval controls your actions. It means that you consider others' opinions more important than your own.

Another mistake people often make is *comparing them-selves with others*. This is a fruitless and demoralizing exercise as, to quote the wisdom of *Desiderata*, 'Always there will be greater and lesser people than yourself'. Human beings were designed to complement each other in a rich mosaic of talents and abilities and you can learn something from everyone you meet. Each of us is different and we all have our individual combination of attributes necessary to fill our particular niche in the overall scheme of things. The only person you should compare yourself with is *you*. Are you making the most of your talents and abilities? Are you meeting your own standards of thinking and behaviour? If not, it's rather like not bothering to open a beautifully wrapped gift that somebody took a lot of time and trouble to choose especially for you.

Never be daunted by someone else's success. By all means admire them for their achievements, but don't say 'I'll never be as good as that'. At some stage that person whom you so admire probably felt very much like you do now. They also looked at another's success in the field and wondered if they could ever match up. But they didn't let it stop them from trying. A person with high self-esteem will feel happy with themselves even if they don't succeed. They respect themselves simply for giving it their best shot.

So much is a man worth
as he esteems himself.

François Rabelais

Social Skills

If your self-esteem is high, you'll have no problem admitting to yourself that you might need to improve your skills in some areas. Social skills are among the most important. If you've been sending out the wrong signals, it's time to make some changes.

Dave stared in alarm at the pizza which had just been served to him. A yell from one of the children confirmed his suspicions. 'Dad, there's meat in the pizzas!'

Dave and his family, all committed vegetarians, were enjoying an evening out in a local restaurant, but when the order arrived, he was momentarily taken aback. Once, his immediate impulse would have been to tell the family to pick out the offending pieces and leave it at that. But not now. He called the waiter. The manager was summoned, profuse apologies were made, dishes were whisked away, fresh (strictly vegetarian) pizzas were hastily prepared and lay sizzling on everyone's plates within 20 minutes. What's more, the bill which arrived at the end of the evening bore the legend, 'No charge. Hope you enjoyed your meal.' Dave sailed out of the restaurant. Once again, assertiveness had worked like a charm.

Of course, assertiveness and self-esteem go hand in hand. If you make an effort to assert yourself, it will, as in Dave's case, boost your self-esteem immensely. Likewise, when you raise your self-esteem, you will find it much easier to assert yourself.

Self-assertion does not mean aggression. It is the knack of stating your case calmly but firmly and making your standards and expectations clear to all concerned, without either treading unnecessarily on any toes or running the risk of being treated like a doormat. If you don't make the effort to assert yourself, *you* will be the loser. The 'easy' way out will cause more problems in the long run. There will always be that nagging 'I wish I'd said . . .' feeling in the back of your mind. You will feel frustrated and angry with yourself, and your self-esteem will slide even lower. You might begin to find that all your decisions are being made for you.

Assertion *can* and *should* be learned, for the sake of your mental and physical health. The very act of expressing your feelings is therapeutic. Always state your case quietly and firmly, without hysterics or uncontrolled emotion. Aim to be direct and stick to your point of view if you believe you are right. People will respect you for this. However, be willing to compromise, if necessary. Your attitude will immediately command respect and attention.

Don't forget, you get treated the way you teach others to treat you. If you want to be treated differently, give out different messages. People are only responding to the signals you're sending them – reflecting back your opinion of yourself.

In a nutshell, self-assertion is important because:

- Your self-esteem and positivity are raised and you feel in control
- Tension, frustration and bottled anger are reduced
- Your mental and physical health are improved
- You are less likely to lose friends through conflict and aggression because you will approach potential problem areas with quiet but firm assurance
- You will not only improve existing relationships but also attract new people into your life
- You will be able to express yourself forcefully but tactfully so that you never offend.

Also, don't forget humour. Humour is a natural tension-buster. A good laugh has defused many a tricky situation, and you should not hesitate to lighten your assertive approach whenever it seems appropriate. It doesn't detract from your assertiveness. In fact, a light-hearted attitude carries a charm all of its own. It helps build rapport, strengthens communication and totally disarms the other person – in the nicest possible way.

To build your assertiveness, think of some areas of your life where you would like to be more commanding. Go into Alpha and visualize yourself being strong and assertive. Do this on a regular basis.

The Art of Saying 'No' (and Making it Sound Like a Compliment)

It's such a little word, and yet we so often have a problem with it, whether it's to a salesperson, colleague at work, friend, child or marriage partner. Most of us want people to like us, so we instinctively try to please by being helpful. Nothing wrong with that of course, so long as it's within reason.

As a child you might have been taught to 'put others first'. This has some merit, in that it discourages selfishness, but the trouble comes when you do it to your own detriment. It is so easy to over-commit yourself, which inevitably means you won't be able to cope. Your stress level will rocket and your self-esteem will plummet. You will also end up having to let people down, wasting their time and your own, and be worse off than before. People will always respect someone who quietly says, 'Thanks, but no thanks'.

Remember, being asked a favour does not mean you're under any obligation whatsoever. If anyone's at a disadvantage, it's the other person, not you. It's your right to say 'no' if you so wish. And it can be done very skilfully.

- If you really think an explanation is warranted, list your reasons by all means, but you are not otherwise obliged to do so.
- Don't change your mind unless you want to.
- Be firm, not aggressive.
- Soften your answer, so as not to offend: 'I always love your parties and I'm sorry I can't make it.' 'That's a wonderful offer but I'm afraid it's not feasible at present.'

Lastly, if you are undecided, take time to think it over. Don't let yourself be manipulated by emotional blackmail. Again, use humour if appropriate.

Handling Criticism

It's always the most famous and successful people who are subjected to the worst onslaughts of criticism and ridicule, hence the popularity of satirical magazines and television programmes. So if you find you're criticized a lot, congratulations! You've arrived! The last thing you should ever let it do is bother you. Your critics probably have their own dark motives anyway, which have little to do with your actions or personal qualities. People who are always criticizing others are usually very critical of themselves and invariably attract lots of criticism from others.

This does not, of course, apply to genuine appraisal: constructive criticism given by someone who is in a position to teach and advise. So before you react, first determine whether the criticism is fair. If not, reject it. If on the other hand, it is helpful, be glad that you have someone to guide you, and learn all you can while you have the chance.

Only a person with a very low opinion of themselves is really mortified by criticism. As you build up your confidence, you will learn to put it all in its true perspective. Take what you want and dismiss the rest.

Building the Self-esteem of Others

Never underestimate the value of an encouraging word. It may not mean much to you and you may have forgotten it within half an hour, but the warm feeling you've left behind will remain with the recipient for a long time. If that recipient happens to be a child, so much the better. You could have helped to shape her personality and her future.

I can live for two months
on a good compliment.

Mark Twain

What's more, the Law of Attraction will swing into operation, ensuring that whatever you give out will return to you with interest. When you help someone else feel better about themselves, you feel better about yourself too. It may seem easier to criticize, and it often takes more effort to find somebody's good points, but it is more rewarding both for you and them.

When you pay someone a compliment, somehow some of the glow rubs off on you. So here are some helpful hints.

- Make a point of praising others. Take every opportunity to express your sincerely-felt gratitude, appreciation, acceptance and encouragement. Not indiscriminately, of course, because constant praise can encourage others (especially children) to settle for less than their best, but whenever you feel they've done something to deserve it. Praise their *efforts* rather than their *results*. This way, they are more likely to keep trying.
- When someone speaks to you, pay attention and listen. Stop what you are doing, look at them and paraphrase their words to communicate your understanding to them. Don't just listen – be *seen* to be listening.
- Always keep your word. Never promise anyone anything you either cannot or do not wish to deliver.
- Avoid blaming, ridiculing or judging others and never try to make them feel guilty.
- Avoid destructive criticism and sarcasm at all costs, especially with children. Children are less able to judge whether criticism is fair, and it can result in their never being able to handle criticism as an adult, and perhaps becoming defensive and withdrawn. It doesn't improve their performance – quite the reverse. Often, it leads to their giving up altogether.
- If you feel you have some valid criticisms to make, always criticize the person's *behaviour*, not their character. Say: 'I didn't like the way you did that', rather than: 'You are an idiot. Why are you so stupid?'
- If you are a parent, the most important move you can make to build your child's self-esteem is to work on your own. Most children are, however unwittingly, stripped of their self-esteem by incompetent parents who are themselves lacking in this department, and it is virtually impossible for such parents to instil confidence into their children. High self-esteem is not hereditary, but it can be passed on by example, by parents who have a solid sense of their own

self-worth. Children learn best in three ways: by example, by example and by example.

- Finally, in building a child's self-esteem, it is very important to give her plenty of attention and lots of time. If you spend only a few minutes a day with your children, or are always too busy, they'll soon get the message: 'Mum and Dad don't want to spend any time with me. It must be because I'm not very important. I'm obviously not worth spending time with.' It's a fallacy that a few minutes of so-called 'quality time' make up for a lack of time spent with your children. It doesn't. They desperately need both quality *and* quantity.

People who have consciously raised their self-esteem sometimes find that others take a while to adjust, or even find it threatening. So you might have to allow your colleagues and loved ones time to get used to the new you. Some, masquerading as 'concerned' friends, might even try to knock you back to where you were, but don't fool yourself that they're doing it for your benefit; they're worried about themselves. You'll have to work patiently on teaching them new ways to react to you. If they refuse to learn, perhaps you need to find a new circle of supportive friends.

You owe it to yourself to be the best you possibly can. If you owned a Ferrari, you wouldn't drive it with the brakes on, would you? Similarly, to settle for less than that which you are capable of deliberately reduces your own personal power.

A beggar once stopped a wealthy businessman in the street and asked him for the price of a cup of tea. The businessman was a sympathetic person, and he thought about giving him enough for a meal. He could certainly afford it. However, he reached into his pocket and pulled out some small change. 'If this is all you ask of life', he said to the beggar, 'this is all life will ever give you.'

When you begin to feel confident, you are not afraid to expect the best, to ask for what you want. People will be drawn to you and a whole new world will open up. You are in tune with the Source of Life, the Universal Intelligence itself. Things will often seem to 'fall into place'. You will find it much easier to do whatever you want, and become the person you want to be.

Keep going until you get results, because the techniques we have outlined are not a bag of conjuring tricks. They are the basis of changing your thinking and creating a new life for yourself – one that is rich in health, happiness and success!

17 The Power Within

ALLOW YOURSELF TO BE GUIDED AND SUPPORTED BY THE
UNIVERSAL INTELLIGENCE WITHIN AND YOU WILL ALWAYS BE
HAPPY, HEALTHY AND SUCCESSFUL AND HAVE THE COURAGE TO
FOLLOW YOUR DREAMS.

Dynamic Living Principle 10

The Reverend Arthur Hutt sat at his desk, frowning over
an empty page. How on earth was he going to deliver
an inspiring sermon next Sunday if he couldn't find the
inspiration to write one in the first place? To make matters
worse, little seven-year-old Joe was running amok again. No
doubt the good Lord had his reasons for sending him such a
little tearaway, but there were times when the Reverend came
dangerously close to using some very irreverent language in
his young son's presence. This was one of them.

He leapt to his feet and in desperation tore a page out of a
magazine and ripped it to shreds. 'Here, Joe,' he said, 'let's see
if you can put that together again.' It happened to be a map
of the world and he was confident that he'd bought himself
at least an hour's peace.

Alas, it was not to be. 'I've done it! Come and see!' came
the triumphant cry within a mere 20 minutes. The Reverend's
eyes widened as he inspected the sticky but accurate jumble
of sellotape and paper. 'How did you manage it so quickly?'
he asked.

'Oh, it was easy, Dad!' replied the boy, 'I just turned it
over and there was a man on the other side. When I put
him together, the world fell into place.' Reverend Hutt
thought for a moment. 'Out of the mouths of babes . . . he
muttered, picking up his pen. He began scribbling furiously.

His parishioners still remark on the inspiring sermon he gave one Sunday on the theme: 'Get the man right and his world will be right.'

When the tomb of Hermes was discovered, scholars were waiting to hear the secret of life. They found a single inscription: 'As above, so below. As within, so without.'

If Dave had heard that sermon, it might have saved him many years of frustration and unhappiness. Like many young people, he wanted to change the world, and devoted all his spare time to it. He joined consumer groups, environmental groups, civil rights groups; collected money, distributed leaflets, even stood for Parliament. It certainly kept him busy and gave him something to think about, but still he was not happy. Then it dawned on him. *The cause of his unhappiness lay entirely within himself.* He realized that his own attitude was responsible for his discontent, not what was going on around him.

This didn't mean, of course, that worldwide suffering had been miraculously relieved; but it made him see it in a new light. How could an unhappy person ever create a happy world? It was impossible.

So he started working on himself. He realized that his inner power had been swamped beneath a deluge of negative thoughts and critical judgements about himself and other people. He had been stumbling around in the dark, cut off from his inner guidance, justifying the direction of his life with left-brained logic and material considerations rather than following the dictates of his heart. When he discovered the Dynamic Living Principles, a process of change was begun. He consciously changed his thinking and as his inner power began to awaken his life began to change. At last he felt as if he was heading in the right direction.

Rex, too, has had his fair share of wandering through

an emotional wilderness, and it was only when he became aware of his inner power that his life improved. For years, he struggled and battled. He devoted himself to his practice and his studies, filling his head with facts and figures until his left brain was overloaded, and yet he seemed to be making so little progress towards his cherished ambition of helping millions of people to improve the quality of their lives . . . Then one day a wise and caring friend took him aside and offered him the best advice he'd ever had: 'You try too hard. Stop struggling. Just get yourself in tune with life and all else will follow.'

This started him thinking. He remembered how he'd once asked his teacher how he could best help other people. He'd never forgotten the reply: 'You can't help others unless you're whole first.' It began to dawn on Rex that it was all about harmony of mind, body and spirit. He realized that he'd been like someone wondering why the electrical appliances in his house were not working, and cursing the equipment, when all the time the electricity had been switched off at the mains. Switch on, and everything bursts into life! Nothing works if we are disconnected from our Source.

Rex's friend's advice brought about a remarkable transformation. His business improved. New ideas flourished. Suddenly, he seemed to have more friends. He laughed and smiled more. His relationship with his children improved. So did his health. He felt an all-encompassing sense of peace. He had learned to let go and 'go with the flow'.

'Going with the flow' means realizing that you don't have to be in control of every part of your life all the time and allowing your inner power to guide you. It is a quantum leap of faith, accepting the trials and tribulations of human existence and trusting that everything is taken care of and ultimately works out for your benefit.

It's very much like the 'Magic Eye' pictures which at first glance appear to be a random assortment of coloured blobs, but if you relax your eyes and allow them to go hazy, and then fix your gaze for long enough, an image eventually appears. The shift in consciousness that takes place in the 'magic eye' of your mind is not necessarily dramatic, more like a gradual awakening. 'Ah yes,' you say to yourself, 'now I see it!'

But first you must cast off your old, negative beliefs, allow both sides of your brain to work in harmony to their full capacity and access your inner wisdom – the essence of this book. And you can do it. You now have the basic toolkit – but you will only succeed if you use it. If you dedicate yourself to this exciting quest, and persevere, you *will* change yourself and your life.

Nothing we ever imagine is beyond our powers;
only beyond our present self-knowledge.

Theodore Roszak

The fog will clear and your own 'magic eye' picture will sharpen into focus and you will then be ready for the fifth and final element of the Dynamic Living Formula, the 'as if' principle.

Reflect for a moment. Who are you? Where did you really come from? Why are you here? Are you the result of nothing more than a random accident, as some scientists would have us believe, or is there a pattern? Scientists once tried to calculate the probability that the universe could have been brought into existence by a series of random and uncoordinated events, and found the odds against it so overwhelming that even the most advanced computer couldn't handle the calculations. Every society down the ages has recognized that there must be some Intelligence operating through us. It doesn't matter what you call it. It created you, nurtures you and takes care of your emotional and spiritual needs. It provides for you all your life, if you allow it to.

Live as if this Intelligence is working through you. Express it in your day-to-day activities and life takes on new meaning. Have the courage to trust in it and it will never let you down.

Try this 30-day programme: for one month, live as if you are at one with the Source and 'go with the flow'. Learn to expect the best all the time. Consider everything as a learning experience, which works out perfectly whatever happens. Simply trust and apply Dynamic Living Principle number 8:

LIVE IN THE PRESENT MOMENT. LIFE IS A JOURNEY
TO BE ENJOYED, NOT A STRUGGLE TO BE ENDURED.

Dynamic Living Principle 8

This is what we call 'living dynamically', holding thought patterns of confidence, success and happiness, knowing that you are at one with the power within. It is not about making life easier in a superficial way, but about coping better by developing your inner strength. Living dynamically means you are more relaxed. Your right brain functions more effectively. Your intuition steps up a gear, and answers to seemingly impossible problems appear. And from this new, tranquil centre within you radiates a special charm that attracts people. You become a magnet for others seeking the same peace of mind and sense of purpose that you have. In fact, you find you attract whatever you need into your life effortlessly and naturally. You have awakened 'the power within'.

So where do you go from here? How are you going to use this knowledge?

As we said earlier in this book, most people operate at less than 10 percent of their true potential, but there is no reason why you should be one of them. Health, happiness and success are available to all, and, like the inscription in the tomb of Hermes, the 'secrets' of which we write are nothing new: they have been known ever since the dawning of civilization thousands of years ago. As Henry Thoreau said, 'If you can head confidently in the direction of your dreams and live the kind of life you have imagined, you will come across a success undreamt of in common hours.'

Rex recently attended the UK Royal National Institute for the Blind 'Business Person of the Year' awards in London. He was struck by the power and astonishingly enduring courage of the human spirit. Despite their physical limitations, all the competitors were cheerful and good humoured. Although some had spent a lifetime in total darkness, they had found a source of strength inside themselves which spurred them on. There could only be one first prize, but the judges expressed their opinion that all were winners in their own special way.

For example, one couple – both totally blind – had travelled to London by train, then navigated themselves across the city by Underground train and taxi (a journey that would have deterred many sighted people), with no help apart from their guide dog. The husband had been made redundant two years earlier, but rather than feeling sorry for himself, had phoned his wife with the news and said 'We're not going to let this get us down, are we?' Their fledgeling business was already going well and won them second prize.

Another participant, who was deaf as well as blind, had opened her own employment and communications agency to help others. And the overall winner was blinded after a battle against leukemia many years before. His wife had recently died of cancer. He had built up, and sold, two previous companies and was now helping people to build their own homes. He designed and sold 50 houses a year and used a large workforce of previously unemployed people to build them. It worked out very economically. Clearly, many sighted people would have been daunted by such a challenge.

In contrast, we all know of people with all their faculties who fritter away their time and energy. One of Rex's patients told him of her stepson, a young man in his early 20s in reasonably good health, who lies in bed all day, drinking, smoking and watching television. He justifies his behaviour by asserting that 'there is no point in making an effort because the world will end sometime'. Many people slide into a state of apathy and emptiness, waiting for a 'lucky break' but doing little to help themselves. They have no energy, no motivation, no sense of meaning or direction in their lives. Why?

The answer is simple. Attitude. With the wrong attitude, you are cut off from your Source. To recall the famous statement by William James, you can change your life by changing your attitude. Such a simple step. As the Bible says, 'Where there is no vision, the people perish'. Who is lacking vision – the blind people who *cannot* 'see' but who overcome tremendous obstacles to make a success of their lives, or those who *will not*. The former lack eyesight but the latter lack something far more disabling. Who is the more handicapped?

And now, it's up to you. Create the kind of life you want. You have all the tools. Inspire yourself, and be an inspiration to others. Awaken your inner power. Allow it to express itself through you. Light up your own life and light up the world!

There is not enough darkness in all the world to extinguish the light of even one small candle.

Robert Alden

Appendix: The Dynamic Living Institute

The Dynamic Living Institute was founded by Rex Johnson, David Swindley, Joanne Figov and Colleen Johnson to help people transform their lives, enjoy health, happiness and success and learn to access and release their inner power to live the kind of life they want.

Why 'dynamic' living? 'Dynamic' means activity. We teach ways of improving your life by taking action, and especially by making the best use of your most important resource – your mind.

We have studied and researched this for more than 20 years, distilling and integrating the techniques of the best brains in the field. To this we have added and incorporated our own experience in holistic health, education, business, hypnotherapy and psychotherapy.

In addition to writing books and pamphlets, we also offer the 'Dynamic Living Programme' (see below), give talks and workshops wherever there is a demand, run short courses for business and sports organizations, and offer individual counselling.

For further details, contact: The Dynamic Living Institute, 45A Branksome Wood Road, Bournemouth, BH4 9JT, United Kingdom, telephone 01202 762202.

The Dynamic Living Programme

The Dynamic Living Programme is a 12-month course, each monthly unit comprising:

- a 60-minute instructional tape (which includes a 28-day, habit-changing programme) which can be used over and over again;

- a relaxation tape (which works at an unconscious level);
- informative study notes;
- an assessment sheet to help you monitor your progress.

Participants who complete the programme receive a certificate to mark their achievement and are eligible to train as accredited DLP Personal Development Facilitators.

The same course is also available as three, 4-monthly units.

1 **Awaken Your Inner Power.** The foundation course which includes: tapping into your inner wisdom; using the power of positive thinking; creative imagery and affirmations; and creating confidence.
2 **Living Dynamically.** Making a success of the material side of life, including: developing a prosperity consciousness; defining and accomplishing goals; handling stress constructively; and listening and communication skills.
3 **Feeling Good All The Time.** Enjoying good health, happiness and peace of mind on a mental, emotional and spiritual level, covering: the three cornerstones to health; self-healing; taking charge of the emotions; building fulfilling relationships (with yourself and others); and exploring the connection between mind, body, spirit and the Universal Intelligence.

Units are also available individually.

Further Reading

Dyer, Dr Wayne, *Pulling Your Own Strings*, Arrow Books, 1988
 —*Your Erroneous Zones*, Warner, 1992
Field, Lynda, *Creating Self-Esteem*, Element Books, 1983
Frankl, Victor, *Man's Search for Meaning: An Introduction to Logotherapy*, Beacon Press, 1962
Gawain, Shakti, *Creative Visualisation*, Bantam Books, 1978
Hay, Louise, *The Power is Within You*, Eden Grove, 1991
Helmstetter, Shad, *What to Say When You Talk to Yourself*, Thorsons, 1991
Hill, Napolean, *Think and Grow Rich*, Ballantine, 1990
Holland, Ron, *Talk and Grow Rich*, Thorsons, 1989
Johnson, Rex and David Swindley, *Creating Confidence – The Secrets of Self-Esteem*, Element Books, 1994
Lindenfield, Gael, *Assert Yourself*, Thorsons, 1992
McWilliams, John-Roger and Peter, *You Can't Afford the Luxury of a Negative Thought*, Thorsons, 1990
Murphy, Joseph, *The Power of Your Subconscious Mind*, Pocket Books, 1995
Peale, Norman Vincent, *The Power of Positive Thinking*, Mandarin, 1990
Peiffer, Vera, *Positive Thinking*, Element Books, 1989
Robbins, Anthony, *Unlimited Power*, Simon and Schuster, 1986
Segal, Bernie, *Love Medicine and Miracles*, Random House, 1986
Silva, Jose and Burt Goldman, *The Silva Mind Control Method of Mental Dynamics*, Grafton Books, 1988
Simonton, Carl and Stephanie, *Getting Well Again*, Bantam Books, 1980

Index

Abrahamson, Leonard 131
accelerated learning 57
acceptance 124, 127–8
action 11, 14, 48, 67, 105, 131–2
Adler, Alfred 29
affirmations 77, 83–90, 93, 101,
    109–10, 127, 129
Alden, Robert 151
Alpha level/state 40–1, 44–5, 48,
    50–1, 56–7, 67, 69, 85, 101,
    108, 126, 129, 133
anchoring 106–108, 133–4
approval 124, 131, 136
Archimedes 53
'As If' principle 148
assertiveness 138–9
attitudes 21–2, 30, 60, 86, 97, 105,
    117, 124, 128–30, 151
Attraction, Law of 98, 141
Aurelius, Marcus 60
autogenics 44
autosuggestion 85, 90, 104, 130
awareness 47, 65–7, 124–7

Bannister, Dr Roger 95, 105
behaviour 22, 117, 124, 142
Behaviourists, the 17, 19, 20, 23
Belief, Law of 102, 118
beliefs 21–2, 30, 117–18,
    120, 126–7
Bible 11, 60, 151
brain 23–4, 105
    left and right hemispheres 36,
        39–40, 50–1, 57, 66–9, 98,
        101, 149
Branden, Dr Nathaniel 22

Bryan, William Jennings 89
Buddha 23
Butler, Samuel 49

Capra, Frank 51
Carlyle, Thomas 60
Cause and Effect, Law of 60–1,
    63, 98, 128
childhood/children 18–21, 142–3
Churchill, Winston 32
Cole Whittaker, Terry 121
conditioning vii, 18–20, 74,
    117–18, 124
conscious thought stopping
    69–71, 129
Couc, Emil 83
creative imagery 84, 90–111,
    127, 130
critical censor 26, 101
criticism 140–1

Dali, Salvador 32
Darrow, Clarence 114
de Quincey, Thomas 55
Law of Desire 102
Dynamic Living Formula xvi,
    111, 148
Dynamic Living Institute xv,
    15, 42, 152
Dynamic Living Principles xvi, 77,
    123, 146
Dynamic Living Programme
    xv, 152–3

Edison, Thomas E 49–50
Einstein, Albert 32, 37, 101

Emerson, Ralph Waldo 32, 61
emotions 30, 59, 88, 104, 106,
    119–20, 126, 133
Expectancy, Law of 102, 110

firewalk 89–90
five A's, the 124–32
five P's, the 86, 89, 129
formulas for failure, five 12–15
Fox, Emmett 70
Frankl, Viktor 28–9
Freud, Sigmund 17, 24, 27, 29, 37

Gandhi, Mahatma 118
Gates, Elmer 49
Gawain, Shakti 111
George, Henry 64
Gibran, Kahlil xv
Gilbert, W.S. 124
goals 86, 101

habits 22, 30
happiness 23, 112, 144, 149
Hay, Louise 100
health 4, 11, 23, 41, 102, 112,
    138–9, 144, 149
Helmstetter, Shad 75
Hermes, tomb of 146, 149
Higher Self 33, 50, 54, 74
Hill, Napolean 50
Holland, Ron 50
Holmes, Oliver Wendell xv
Hopkins, Mark 86
Howe, Elias 52–3
Hugo, Victor xiv
Humanists (school of psychology)
    27
Huxley, Aldous 13
hypnosis 25, 114

ideals 30
ideas 30
insight 67, 91
internal dialogue (see also self talk)
    64, 79, 129

intuition 32–9, 42, 50, 53–4, 149
Isaiah 123

James, Prof. William ix, 151
Jung, Carl Gustav 17, 25,
    27, 37, 40

leisure 12, 113
Lennon, John 2
life areas, the 11–12
Living Dynamically 149
Locke, John 52
Lozonov, Dr Georgi 57, 94

Mansell, Nigel 115
Maslow, Abraham 4, 17, 27–8
McGinnis, Alan Loy 134
meaning, search for 28–9
memory, memories 30, 35, 54–6
memory affirmation 56
Mental Diet, Seven Diet 70–2
mental rehearsal 93, 130, 134
Milton, John 19
mind 17, 20, 23, 29–31, 73
    collective unconscious 37–8,
        49–50
    conditioned 67–9
    conscious 24, 26, 85, 99,
        107, 127
    reflective 67–9
    unconscious 21, 24–5, 32, 38,
        49–50, 52, 54, 63, 76–7, 85,
        88, 97–101, 104, 106–107, 127
mindfulness 65–7, 129
mindpower 49–58
mirror of the mind 105–106, 130
modelling 132–3
Molière x
Montagne, Michel Eyquem 64
motivation 26–8
Mozart, W.A. 33

Niebuhr, Reinhold 128
Nightingale, Earl 60

Ornish, Dr Dean 96

parents/parenting 20–1, 122, 142
Pavlov, Ivan 20
peace of mind 5, 41, 149
Penfield, Dr Wilder 54–5
physiology, positive 132
Plato 74
pleasure and pain 26–8, 68
Projection, Law of 98
Prover, the 63–4, 72–4, 76, 79, 129
Psycho-neuro-immunology 97

questions, positive 79, 81, 129
quick relaxants 45–7

Rabelais, François 137
reframing 108, 126
relationships 5, 6, 11, 86, 101,
  113, 135
relaxation 25, 39–48, 78, 86, 111,
  129, 134
  differential 42–3
  progressive 43–4
Rochefoucauld, La 40
Rogers, Dr Carl 17
Roosevelt, Eleanor 135
Roszak, Theodore 148
Rousseau, Jean-Jacques 17
Royce, Josiah 66
Rushmore, Mount 92
Russell, Dr Bertrand 51

Schuller, Robert 7
Schultz, Dr Johannes 44
Segal, Dr Bernie 95
self-esteem 6, 112–44
self-image 108
  six types of 119–21
self-talk 74–7, 111, 129, 131
Shakespeare, William 60, 132

Shaw, George Bernard 96, 110
sigh breath 46
Simonton, Drs Carl and Stephanie
  96
Singer, Isaac Bashevis 73
sitting for ideas 50–2
sleeping on it 52–3
social skills 137–41
Socrates 15
Somerset-Maugham, W 11
Source (of life) vii, 33, 72, 74, 144,
  147, 149, 151
Sperry, Prof. Roger 36
Steinem, Gloria 112
success 23, 135, 144, 149
suggestion, power of 84–5
Sweetland, Ben 94
Swish technique 106, 130

Thatcher, Margaret 136
Thinker, the 63–4, 72, 76
thinking/thoughts 6, 13, 17–18,
  31, 59–82, 88, 91, 97, 124,
  131, 146
Thoreau, Henry David 7, 149
thumb and finger technique 56
Twain, Mark 3, 141

Universal consciousness 38, 49
Universal Intelligence, the xvi, 23,
  38, 50, 57, 72, 100, 110, 144

visualization, see creative imagery
Voltaire 100

Waitley, Dr Dennis 116
Watson, J.B. 17, 19
Watson, James 23
West, Mae 108
Wilde, Oscar 117
wordpower 77–9, 129